# CONTENT TO CLIENTS

Build, Market & Sell Your Service on
Social Media in 9 Simple Steps

CHRIS JAMES

Copyright © Chris James, 2024

ISBN 978-1-915962-51-5
Published by Compass-Publishing UK

Cover artwork by © Benedicto Cernall III
Cover photography © David Moss
Back cover photography © Thomas Jackson
Diagrams © Chris James

Edited and designed by The Book Refinery Ltd
www.TheBookRefinery.com

All rights reserved. This book or any portion thereof may not be reproduced or used in any manner whatsoever without the express written permission of the publisher except for the use of brief quotations in a book review.

This book contains material designed to assist your business. While the author has made every effort to verify that the information provided in this book is correct and up to date, the author assumes no responsibility for any error, inaccuracy or omission.

The advice, examples and strategies contained herein are not suitable for every situation. The materials contained herein are not intended to represent or guarantee you will achieve your desired results, and the author shall not be liable for damages arising there from. Success is determined by a number of factors beyond the control of the author, including, but not limited to, market conditions, the capital on hand, effort levels and time.
You understand every individual business carries an inherent risk of capital loss and failure.

*This book is dedicated to my little family: Amy, Ivy and Edward.*

*Love you guys.*

*It's also written in memory of my father and brother-in-law; may they rest in peace.*

# About Chris James

No good salesperson talks about themself first.

So I'll see you on page 265 after you've read this book.

*You don't need to be a salesperson – you need to be a person who sells.*

— Zoe Whitman

# Foreword
## By Zoe Whitman

I closed a business because my leads dried up.

There's a longer story that involves a global pandemic, kids under three and losing a heap of clients practically overnight, but the reason my business wasn't going to survive came down to cash flow. And cash flow came down to this:

**I didn't have a sales pipeline.**

And that was on me.

Fast forward four years, and my business partner (Jo Wood) and I have built a huge, loyal community filled with our ideal clients.

The business employs us both and our husbands. It allows us to work part-time around our families. We do work we love whilst making an impact.

In this business, building an audience was the easy part. Bookkeeping and accountancy aren't exactly *known* for their social media influencers. But as impressive as our 20k-strong online community sounds, having an audience full of 'raving fans' doesn't guarantee us the lifeblood of every business: sales.

It's not just about eyeballs on content. It's about a system that generates leads. And just as this book will teach you, we've needed to put in the reps.

You will too.

I've been the person who's made excuses:

- I don't have the time.
- I don't have the money.
- I have to do something else first.

In fact, I was the person who took 18 months before I finally accepted the inevitable that I needed Chris's consulting programme, Content to Clients. And by then, I had to convince Chris I should be allowed to join.

I thought I was joining to learn the systems that feel so alien when you're 'not a salesperson', but what makes this special is the mindset.

**You don't need to be a salesperson – you need to be a person who sells.**

Mindset is everything.

So here's the thing…

This book? It's more than words on a page and shit-hot diagrams. It's Chris. It's his brain in a book. It's the journey from questioning your worth to knowing your worth without a doubt.

Chris will give you tough love. He won't sugarcoat it.

But he'll also become your friend – a 'let's randomly go bowling with the kids' kind of friend – because he cares about your family and your business as much as you do. And you'll care about his.

The work you think you need to do? That's *not* the work. The real work is right here in these pages.

- Don't wait 18 months.
- Don't make excuses.
- Don't question whether you're worth it.

You are.

Instead, ask yourself this: Do I back myself?

Because when you do, it doesn't just change your business. It changes your life.

**Zoe Whitman**
**Co-Founder | The 6 Figure Bookkeeper**
**June 2024**

*The main thing is to keep the main thing, the main thing.*

— Stephen R. Covey

# Contents

| | |
|---|---|
| Foreword | 7 |
| Introduction | 13 |
| **Build** | 17 |
| Chapter 1. Offer | 19 |
| Chapter 2. Message | 51 |
| Chapter 3. Traction | 75 |
| *Free Tool: Offer-Building Blueprint* | 101 |
| **Market** | 103 |
| Chapter 4. Journey | 105 |
| Chapter 5. Content | 121 |
| Chapter 6. Leads | 155 |
| *Free Tool: 12 High-Converting Posts* | 183 |
| **Sell** | 185 |
| A Brief Intermission: Sales Psychology | 187 |
| Chapter 7. Discovery | 195 |
| Chapter 8. Pitch | 213 |
| Chapter 9. Objections | 237 |
| *Free Tool: Sales-Call Roadmap* | 259 |
| Conclusion | 261 |
| Final Thoughts | 262 |
| Acknowledgements | 264 |
| About Me | 265 |
| About Contents to Clients (C2C) | 266 |

*There will never be a perfect time to launch your offer.*

# Introduction

As far as I know, there are no books out there that show you how to build an offer, market it using content *and* sell it too.

**Until now.**

This book is the fucking slap around the face I needed when I started my business. And it's the same slap in the face I give to my clients too. (Metaphorically, obviously.)

When I began this journey, there was nothing like this around. Nothing that simplified and packaged the information into one book. If there had been, I might not have done as many stupid things.

Or been as afraid to take as many risks.

If the principles I'm going to share with you in this book had been drilled into me 10 years ago, I'd probably be further along in my career now.

Richer too.

**That's why this book exists: to help give you the knowledge you need to start taking action today.**

I'm going to show you how to take any idea you want, build it, market it *and* sell it.

You don't have to wait 10 years and figure it all out yourself. It's all here ready for you in the coming chapters.

The hardest thing you'll have to do is put it into action. But let's not worry about that right now. Let's just get started.

## Build, market and sell

There are three sections in this book and nine chapters. At the end of each section, you'll find a free tool that'll support the information you've just learned.

| | | | |
|---|---|---|---|
| **Build** | Offer | Message | Traction |
| **Market** | Journey | Content | Leads |
| **Sell** | Discovery | Pitch | Objections |

Whatever stage you're at – whether you're trying to build an offer, market it *or* sell it – you should be able to open up the relevant chapter and find it useful.

### Section 1. Build

Without a good offer, you don't have a business.

So, in this section, we'll start by building one that you can sustain and earn money from. Then you'll learn about creating a message that'll attract the right people.

A lot of people lose motivation after they create their offer, because they don't get the outcomes they hope for or problems come up.

That's why *Chapter 3. Traction* is included; it's to get you over that first bump in the road and get you results, fast.

## Section 2. Market

Once you've built your offer, you need to tell people about it.

You need to learn how to bring eyeballs to your business and how to maintain that attention so you can convert it into sales. We'll explore the customer journey in *Chapter 4*, and you'll discover what a lot of people get wrong and what you can do right.

In *Chapter 5*, you'll learn my approach to creating content, and then we'll finish this section by focusing on how you can start bringing in leads.

## Section 3. Sell

You don't have a business if you don't sell, so this last section is probably the most important. Sales is the most challenging part of running a business too.

The short chapter on sales psychology will reveal some secrets I've learned along the way. And then – in *Chapters 7, 8* and *9* – we'll cover the key points of a successful sales call, plus what you can say and do to ensure you convert the right leads into clients.

This might sound a lot, but by the end of the nine chapters, your business – and your mindset – will be transformed for the better.

But that's enough talking. Let's gooooooo!

# BUILD 1

*Action is where your results are found.
Not in preparation.*

# Chapter 1
# Offer

I don't do fluff, so here goes...

Too many small business owners piss about.

And chances are, you're one of them.

But ask yourself this: who wins?

The person that gets all their polished ducks in a perfect little row first?

Or the person who hits the ground early, taking action in every way possible?

When I first started building my business, I saw a lot of big players and gurus making online courses, all shouting about earning passive income. It made me think I had to start there too.

Plus, I loved pissing around to the nth degree designing carousels, building and planning. I still do. It feels good to be working towards building something rather than selling. Because no one really likes selling, do they?

**In reality, I'd been misled. And so have you.**

What the gurus don't tell you about is the work that actually needs to be done, which is having conversations with people and selling to them.

But if you knew that, it would mean fewer sales for the gurus…

For most people, building landing pages, designing websites and making sure everything looks shiny is a lot more exciting. And it's what sells. It feels productive because there's an instant reward.

**However, that's just a form of *procrastination* and a way of avoiding the real work that needs to be done.**

I spent *weeks* creating an online course and – surprise, surprise – it only sold two copies. I'd built something that wasn't relevant and put it out to an audience that wasn't primed for it.

You can't build an offer on guesswork.

The *solutions* your clients need will come from working *with* them, which means *real-time feedback is crucial* if you want to build something that sells.

Once I realised that, things started to fall into place.

On 3rd January 2022, I launched Content to Clients (C2C), my six-month online consulting programme, with just three people and three training videos inside it. My clients could have consumed everything in under a day. So I worked like mad, building things out as we progressed. If they had questions, I'd make a video or a tool. I listened to their feedback and refined it.

Then I refined it again.

And again.

Even now, I'm still refining C2C. It'll never be finished.

It feels counterintuitive, but you have to build the plane whilst flying it. I promise you that you'll get to your destination faster, and you'll have less turbulence along the way too!

> ***There will never be a perfect time to launch your offer.***

I still have doubts.

Imposter syndrome still creeps in. If you're an entrepreneur, you probably like to procrastinate and perfect things, and chances are you compare yourself to others.

However, there are far too many variables for any of that to be a real comparison, so don't bother.

I mean it.

You've got to keep all those fears in check. Otherwise, you're going to end up telling yourself lies such as 'Oh, I'll just write this list. I need some business cards. I just need one of those neon signs so I look cool on Zoom calls.'

**But think of it like this: every minute you waste avoiding what needs to be done, it'll cost you a day – or maybe even a month – of sales, growth and potential success.**

Someone once said to me, 'I'll monetise when I get to 2k followers.' Why? Why wait? Monetise *now*. Even if you don't make a profit at the start, at least your followers will continue to grow as you build. I had a moment with a client not long ago about this very issue.

'How much progress have you made?' I asked him on one of our catch-up calls.

'None' he said.

'Okay, and how much progress do you think your competitors have made?'

Silence. It was obvious...

Be prepared for uncertainty as you start this journey – and be okay with it. You *will* experience discomfort every single day. So you might as well take action, *regardless* of how you feel and what you think.

### *Action is where your results are found.*
### *Not in preparation.*

I'm under no illusion that I've taken action on lots of the wrong things and wasted shitloads of time, but none of that time is really lost because I had to make those mistakes in order to build C2C. We don't win or lose – we win or learn.

So, let's start moving...

## Building your offer

What's an 'offer'?

An offer is a business solution to a problem. It's *your* solution to a problem or a desire communicated in a way that motivates people to buy it. It describes what it is, how it works, and the price, time and effort people have to invest in order to get a desired outcome. It's something you're an expert in because it's likely you've gone through it yourself.

**But an offer isn't about you.**

The journey your clients go on isn't the reason they'll buy. It isn't about the bells and whistles, the software you use, the videos you've made, the revisions, the edits, or the number of check-in calls.

An offer is about *them*. It's this:

- ✓ Solving *their* pain.
- ✓ Generating *their* desired result(s).
- ✓ Or helping *them* escape a problem.

**They're buying the transformation.**

**They're buying the results.**

## PRO TIP: THE FOUR PS

Whatever you build and sell should lie directly in the middle of these four Ps:

- Profit
- Passion
- Problem
- Past experience

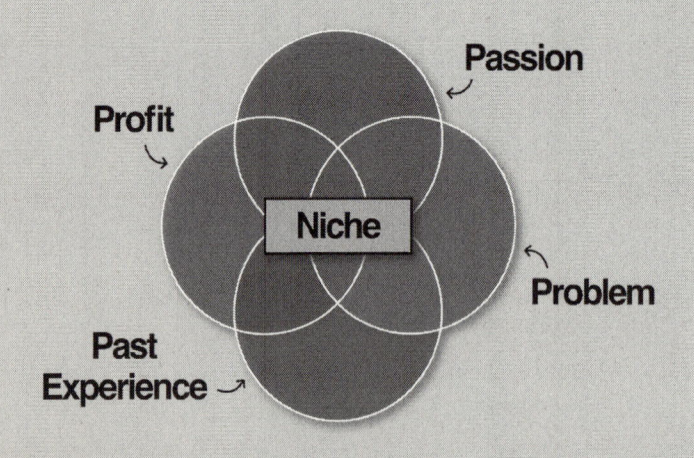

*Passion*
*Profit*
**Niche**
*Problem*
*Past Experience*

It should be something you're passionate about, something you have prior experience in/of, something that solves a problem in the world and something that's profitable too.

A business has to be built to survive the tough times. If you build something that's missing one of these Ps, the chance of success will reduce. So, before we go any further, grab a pad and pen.

I mean it.

Go and get the pad and pen now.

I'm so sick of books that are all theory and no application. I want to inspire action: fast, intentional action.

That's why I want you to brainstorm your four Ps now. Because we're about to dive in and build your offer...

# Build

To build an offer that people want to buy, you have to get clear on – and understand – these six components:

| People | Problems | Promise |
| --- | --- | --- |
| Phases | Parts | Price |

Yes, more words that begin with the letter P:

1. The **people**
2. The **problems**
3. The **promise**
4. The **phases**
5. The **parts**
6. The **price**

I see an offer as being like a music producer mixing a song. You can always turn the hi-hats down, make the bass louder or add in some strings, but a song is never truly finished.

Neither is an offer.

There's always something you can change.

Now isn't the time for that. It's time to commit. Don't worry, you can always fine-tune and change your offer later – *after* you know people want to buy it. But as I said earlier, you have to start doing the work now.

No more waiting.

> I've created a free tool to simplify this whole process for you. Head to the end of *Chapter 3* and download the offer-building blueprint for free.

## 1. The people

The whole process starts with an audience. You need to know and understand your audience because it's no use selling pens to someone who only uses an iPad. It's no use selling UK accounting software to someone in Belgium.

There are a few things that come into play when people decide to buy. But for most people, buying comes from an *emotional* standpoint – how an offer makes them feel – and that's usually related to a problem or desire they have. People need to perceive your product or service to be the answer to their problems.

**Your offer needs to pull on their emotions.**

Of course, it has to make sense to them logically, but when you're aware of the emotional standpoint of your target audience, you'll be in a much stronger position to market to them and help them.

To understand their emotional situation, you can start by writing down the answers to these questions, which will come up in the next few sections:

- → What's their industry or specialism?
- → What's their company size or turnover? Are they solopreneurs?
- → What's their job title(s) and/or department?
- → What's their location?
- → What's their gender and age?
- → What are their likes and dislikes?

List out any other notes or specifics about your target market as well.

You want to get as granular as you can. However, don't worry too much if you don't have all the data to hand; you just need to be 80% happy with it. You could also make a list of people you *don't* want to work with. Are there any locations you want to avoid? Do you want to avoid companies in a particular sector or industry? That can help your thinking as well.

Next, we're going to look at the problem(s) they're facing.

## 2. The problems

As humans, we're never satisfied.

Even though most of us are afraid to change, we all want to change something. And the change people want to create either involves running *away* from pain or running *towards* a desire.

You need to tap into this; in order to sell to people, we need to fully understand their state of pain:

- → What are they running from?
- → What are they running towards?
- → What are the associated roadblocks they're facing?
- → What are the different stages they need to go through to reach their desire?

The gap between where they are now and where they want to be is where you and your offer come into play.

### *You're the key to their transformation.*

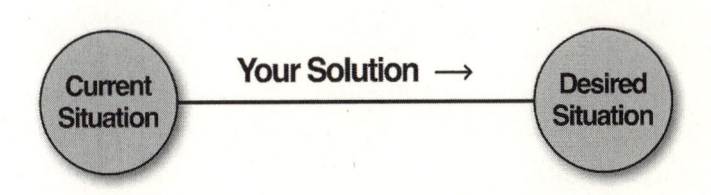

We have to ask ourselves this: what problems do they have? The key here is to be specific. Spend a good bit of time on this and really delve into their minds. Do some research. This isn't just a little list; this is going to inform your whole strategy moving forwards.

**It needs to be solid and robust.**

Block out time in your diary and think about the following:

- → What are they feeling?
- → What are they thinking?
- → What's not working?
- → What will happen if they don't change?
- → What are the consequences if they stay the same as they are?
- → What are the second-order consequences too?

Consider and write down all the logical, emotional and practical pain points.

### PRO TIP: INSIGHT

There are different layers of a problem that you'll need to solve. Most can be put into one of these three categories:

- Health
- Wealth
- Self

> These will be the *emotional* drivers of a purchasing decision. Keep these in mind when you work through this section. We'll cover the emotional reasons why people buy more in the next chapter.

Problems are things such as not having enough time or thinking that LinkedIn isn't a viable channel for marketing. You could list out their limiting beliefs: maybe they fear judgement or have a lack of skills; maybe they've been burned by a past service provider; or maybe they don't even know your solution exists. Write it all down.

If I were to do this for our potential clients, the problems would include these:

- They don't have a clear offer.
- They don't have any/enough leads.
- They don't have systems, workflows or strategies.
- They're not making as much money as they want.
- They feel they're not cut out for business ownership.
- They feel like they need someone to give them permission.

I've taken *hundreds* of calls with clients, and these are just some of the problems people have. There's a much longer list.

You probably know what some of your audience's problems are, but you won't know every single one. That's okay.

If you're unsure what problem to solve for your target market, simply list what you *think* their problem might be, and you can validate it later. We'll cover this in more depth in *Chapter 3*.

### Obstacles

You can also list out the obstacles. What's *stopping* them from achieving the result you can help them get? It could be external constraints (such as other people or their budget) or something internal (such as limiting beliefs or certain behaviours). Maybe they've got a business partner who doesn't do *enough* work? Maybe they have certain habits that prevent them from moving forwards? Is there anything operational or logistical they need to overcome? What are their mental blocks? What time and money constraints do they have? List them all down.

### Solution

Next, let's list out potential solutions. At this stage, you can be quite theoretical. You don't need to actually have the solution right now, just think about *how* the problem *could* be solved.

Look at the elements, services or resources you *could* provide to solve the problem. In what ways *could* you eliminate the roadblock, solve that problem or meet their desire?

It doesn't have to be something you're doing currently; you're looking for things you can provide in the future.

If someone says, 'I don't have enough time,' how can you overcome it? How can your method reduce the time investment dramatically? Can you provide templates, guides and support?

If they have limiting beliefs, what evidence can you give to break those beliefs? If they can't travel to you, can you do online consultations?

> Keep this list safe because these things will be *perfect* for your business-based marketing content, which we'll cover in *Chapter 5*.

What we're doing here is constructing the start of a pitch. We're preparing ourselves for potential objections and ways we could handle them. Remember, nothing here is set in stone. I've seen lots of people stall or fail at the first hurdle because they fear these elements will be tattooed on their forehead.

But don't worry, *you can change and rework this every few months* as you learn more about your target market.

## 3. The promise

This is one of my favourite parts of offer-building. It's a bit like a jigsaw puzzle because you get to play around with a few components to make it sound compelling.

Think of your promise as a mini elevator pitch. It's a really short statement that sums up the various parts of your offer.

When we start working on the message in the next chapter, your promise is going to be essential. It'll inform you what your audience sees, thinks and feels about you. So be specific with your promise, and don't skip over this part.

We don't want your audience in a confused state.

**We want absolute clarity.**

*Simple scales; fancy fails.*

A common mistake people make is trying to cram too much into the promise. When you do this, you risk confusing your clients – and a confused mind never buys. Your promise needs to be as simple as possible. You want to commit to this promise for 90 to 180 days to see how the market responds, and you should only change it once you have feedback and data.

So think about this from your audience's point of view:

- → Where do they want to be?
- → What's going to make their life easier?
- → What's going to remove stress or worry from the problems that you've discovered?

And focus on the *outcome*, not the process. Think of it as selling the *destination*, not the plane journey. (Just like the airlines do in their marketing.)

The following template has been bandied about a lot, but as an initial starting point, you can use it to help you create your promise:

```
I help _____ [audience]

solve _____ [problem] or achieve _____ [outcome]

using _____ [method]

without _____ [pain/frustration]

in _____ [duration].
```

You want them to see that the time, effort and money they invest is going to be worth the desired results. All these parts can be changed and altered, but a good starting point is to look at each of these elements and to write out some variations.

Don't try to fit too much into it.

Remember, you're not tying yourself to this for life. It's not written in blood. But you still want to be as specific as you can. The more words you use, the more potential confusion you might cause, so ignore the urge to justify your promise with fluff.

**Stick to the specifics.**

When I started C2C, our promise was along the lines of this:

> *We help coaches and freelancers [audience] win more clients [outcome] using organic content [method] without ads or complicated funnels [pain] in six months or less [duration].*

Here are a few more examples:

| Pos/Neg | Promise |
|---|---|
| Positive | Helping coaches & freelancers win more clients on social in 4 simple steps. |
| Positive | Coaches & freelancers, use our framework to win 4-figure clients on social. |
| Positive | We help coaches & freelancers win 4-figure clients using organic content. |
| Negative | Coaches, not generating enough leads or clients on social? I can help! |
| Negative | Stuck charging too little for your coaching? Our CTC framework is the answer. |
| Negative | Unsure how to win coaching & freelancing clients using content? We can help. |

Get creative here and move things around to see what works for you. You'll see I've included some positive and some negative variations. I've varied the opening statement and used numbers. I don't use all six criteria for the promise either.

Note down several variations of your promise using a mixture of positive and negative elements, and then pick your favourite one in preparation for the next chapter.

You can use this promise in a few different places. You can drop it into conversation. You can use it on your LinkedIn or Instagram profile. You can use it on your landing pages, on sales calls and even face to face.

**This will evolve.**

Don't worry if it's not where you want it yet; we're just making a start.

## 4. The phases

Now you need to think about the journey that a client goes through when they work with you.

If you had to describe the whole process of taking them on board and helping them solve each of those problems in a specific sequential order, what would that journey look like?

Whether you have 12 steps or 147, you need to simplify that process for your ideal client.

Too much information can bore people and cause them to tune out.

I've found it best to categorise those steps into three easy-to-understand, sequential phases. Doing this will help potential clients to visualise both what it would be like to work with you and the end result, which is absolutely key.

My favourite example is inspired by a van I was stopped behind at a roundabout. I thought the simple message they'd written on the back of their van was brilliant because it spelled out exactly what they did in three phases. Had I not been into marketing or running C2C, maybe I wouldn't have noticed. But for them to explain what they do in such a simple and clear way was too good not to share.

Their phases are **design, build** and **maintain.**

Design · Build · Maintain

First, you work with them to design the thing; next, they build it for you; and then, they maintain it for you. It's so simple and easy to understand. Start thinking about how you can simplify your process and put it in an order that'll be compelling for your target market.

What are the three major milestones you're going to walk through with your client?

For C2C, our three phases are these:

**Offer → Marketing → Sales**

Obviously, there will be several components that make up each of your phases, but keep them nice and wide; you can get granular later. If you have a four- or five-step process, that's absolutely fine too – but the human brain *loves* the number three, so keep things concise.

Finally, think about what objections or blockers occur when your ideal client looks at each of these stages:

→ What common mistakes could they make at each phase?
→ What false information do you see other people giving out in the industry about each of your phases?
→ What limiting beliefs do people have about each of the phases?

Write them down next to your phases. Here's what ours look like:

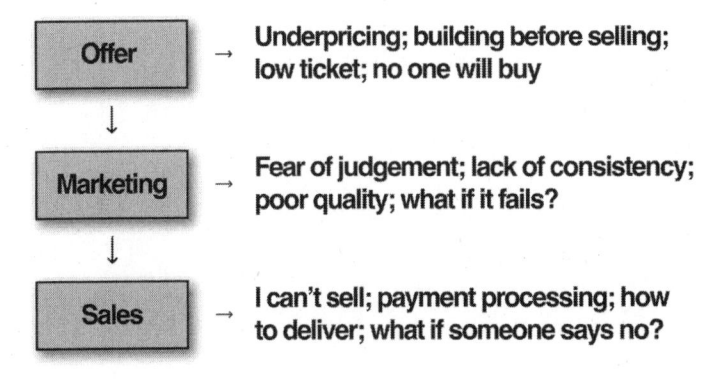

**Offer** → **Underpricing; building before selling; low ticket; no one will buy**

↓

**Marketing** → **Fear of judgement; lack of consistency; poor quality; what if it fails?**

↓

**Sales** → **I can't sell; payment processing; how to deliver; what if someone says no?**

**It's handy to be able to articulate the reason you do things in this order. You want to demonstrate how you're *different*.**

You want to point out the mistakes, errors, limiting beliefs and objections people have and to show them how you'll solve them. Draw from the list of problems you made earlier to help you.

## 5. The parts

If your promise is your outcome plus your method, and the phases are the journey the clients go through, then the parts are what they get. Either *physical, digital or both*. The nuts and bolts.

These are deliverables such as resources, support, bonuses or extras.

This is what most businesses *think* their clients care about, but it's actually what they care the *least* about.

If the promise is clear and the phases describe an easy journey, they don't care *how* you deliver the outcome, *so long as they achieve it!*

All they want to know is this: can this person/business get me to where I want to go?

But even though the parts are the smallest piece of your offer, you shouldn't ignore them. They're still valuable because they allow you to increase the perceived chance of success.

Instead of selling your offer as separate things, it's best to give people an all-encompassing solution, and one that involves a main deliverable, alongside support, resources and bonuses.

When you offer better, more robust and more well-thought-out parts, you give your audience the feeling of a much more rounded solution.

Here's an example:

If you're a copywriter, saying you'll provide 10 social posts a month isn't exactly compelling. But if you're a copywriter who provides analytics reports, access to a secret podcast and direct message (DM) access 24/7 alongside a monthly strategy session, the offer suddenly sounds much more exciting.

If you're a personal trainer, just delivering your PT sessions online isn't going to help you stand out. But if you provide access to an online community, a free session for every milestone reached, nutritional advice, special offers on supplements, a yearly subscription to MyFitnessPal, a sleep-tracking Oura ring and maybe a free T-shirt – now your offer is a lot more enticing.

Here are some examples and ideas:

| Main Element | Support | Resources | Bonus/Extra |
| --- | --- | --- | --- |
| Group coaching / mastermind | Regular support calls | Course | Masterclass / mini-course |
| 1:1 / private coaching | Community | Cheatsheet, guide, podcast, content calendar | Physical items |
| Design, site build, copywriting, video | DM / email / messenger access | Secret podcast | Analytics / reporting |
| Face to face / retreat | Voice note access | Call recordings / dashboard | Subscription |
| Corporate training / consultancy | SOS calls | Weekly tips / prompts | Guest / expert sessions |

Anyone can offer 'support calls' or 'community access', so in order to enhance your offer, filter your parts through the eyes of a seasoned marketer to make them sound value-packed and unique.

**Spice it up.**

If I tell you C2C has a group call every Tuesday, it doesn't sound very exciting. But when I say, 'We have twice-weekly planning calls, which are your frequent touchpoints with me and the team. There, we help you solve any issues in real time. We use these to hold you accountable so you aren't alone,' the value of those group calls goes up immediately.

When you filter the parts through your marketer's lens, it becomes harder to compare yourself to another person who offers the same service.

Imagine this:

You're a coach on a sales call, and you say you offer a 12-week coaching plan.

The inevitable question comes: 'How much is it?'

Without demonstrating the value, the default measure becomes the price. And when you're judged solely on price, it's a race to the bottom.

Now, imagine this:

You offer a 12-week coaching plan. It has twice-weekly sessions and a monthly SOS call. Clients can send voice notes to you anytime through WhatsApp, and they have access to additional materials 24/7 through an online portal.

Your offer is now much more rounded and unique. Suddenly, price isn't the sole measure of value, and you stand out.

Filter your parts through a marketer's lens and start playing with ways you can communicate the nuts and bolts of your offer in an exciting way. The more *value* there is on offer, the more *exciting* it sounds, and the *higher the perception of success* from your client's point of view.

### PRO TIP: DELIVERY MODELS

There are three models you can use to deliver your service and they each have their own advantages and disadvantages. You can fulfil your solution through a done-for-you (DFY) model, a done-with-you (DWY) model or a do-it-yourself (DIY) model.

**DFY:** This model is harder to scale and high touch. It requires more time from you, and it's a little bit harder to productise. Typically, it needs a person to create or do something consistently.

The client expects big results, it'll probably be priced higher than the other models, and therefore it'll require more effort to win clients. However, you'll probably have higher client loyalty and can actually charge a higher price too.

**DWY:** This requires less of your time. Some elements are scalable, and the clients will still expect results. It's medium touch, but it might require a discovery call to sell. The good thing about this is that you can choose the time you put into it, and you'll learn a hell of a lot whilst you're delivering it.

**DIY:** This is the model most people mess around with, and it's usually in the form of trying to sell a course online to get that passive income. I stay away from this because I've tried it and failed. Unless you've got thousands of followers or loads of traffic, the DIY model won't work as effectively as most people think.

DIY is harder to sell, and there's less chance of completion if the client is fully reliant on themselves. It usually sits at a lower price point, which means you don't make as much money.

The pros are that it's low touch, the client will expect less (or nothing) of you, and you can automate a lot of it. It's easy to template or productise, you can scale the hell out of it, and it doesn't take up much time after the initial set-up (bar some admin). But I suggest staying away from a DIY model for now.

## 6. The price

We've all got a certain type of relationship with money: our 'money mindset'. We all have a perception of ourselves, how we should be and what we're worth, and all these things will be reflected in the price we charge.

When I started my side hustle, I charged £80 an hour simply because that was what the agency I worked at charged their clients. I had no concept of what my expertise was worth.

Then, someone told me I should charge £2.5k for a package. The next sales call I had, I nervously quoted £2.5k…

…and the lady paid me in full on the call.

**I was like, *'Holy shit.'***

You'll be inclined to charge less than you're worth when you're just starting out. However, clients *will* pay your ideal price if their perception of the experience and the outcome is compelling enough.

This is why it's so important to have a strong promise, plus understandable phases and parts.

Undercharging or using hourly rates is easier. No doubt about it. You can stay in your comfort zone, and it might seem easier to find clients. There are benefits to incentive-based or beta pricing when you're testing the market.

But when you undercharge, you're shooting yourself in the foot.

**When you try to compete in that low-price arena, you'll be judged solely on what you cost, rather than the value you bring.**

It means your relationships with your clients become transaction-based rather than value-based.

If you charge hourly, you allow people to itemise your time. And when people itemise, they scrutinise. You attract bargain hunters, micro-managers and a lot of headaches. Essentially, you become an employee because you're being paid for your time when you should be paid for your expertise and the outcome.

If you're good at what you do, the impact of your work is potentially priceless.

**So you need to charge for the *impact you have*.**

When you start to think about pricing like this, it'll change the game. I speak to coaches who've been going for five years or more who still charge by the hour or by the day.

Not acceptable.

***Start to consider* impact-*based pricing: charging based on the impact you're going to create for your client rather than the input you give.***

I've seen a common legend online about the price of selling a service, which reframes pricing perfectly:

*Turning one screw is £1.*

*But having the knowledge and experience to know which screw to turn is £9,999.*

So the important question is this: what *should* you charge? I can't say, because only you know the impact you create for your client. To help, do a bit of research as to what your competitors are charging. Speak to people who've already paid for something similar. But you'll have to play around with this – as with everything – and find out what works for you.

To give you an idea, I originally priced C2C at £2k. Then once I had proof of concept and was generating some client results, I gradually increased the price.

The following are three different price types to consider. As with everything, these aren't set in stone. You can change them any time you want.

### 1. Your full price

This is the *ideal* amount you want to sell your offer for. I suggest starting high, so pick a number that scares you but is also relative to the transformation or the results that you provide.

I recommend that our service-providing clients start with a four-figure price. Ideally £1.5k–£2k and above, but it all depends on the services you offer.

## 2. Your introductory price

If you're just starting your business or perhaps building a new offer, this is a price you could use to get your first few clients.

If money isn't the immediate objective for you, you can charge a bit less. I still suggest four figures because clients will value it a lot more, but if you have any insecurities about charging more than £2k, bring this down slightly for the first few people. Don't make money a barrier to entry at the start. You just want client results. Lots of them.

Choose a *realistic* price point, but something that's slightly *out of your comfort zone*.

## 3. Your on-call 'incentive' price

You'll have experienced this if you've been on a sales call with me or the team. We offer an incentive rate for people who take action on the call. If that doesn't feel comfortable for you, you could offer a seven-day price or on-call bonuses as an incentive too.

The goal of the incentive price is to inspire *fast* or *immediate* action.

## PRO TIP: MINDSET

*Become* the type of person you want to attract.

I speak to coaches on sales calls who want to charge £5k for their programme, and yet they won't pay £5k for someone else's. Even with all the blockers removed, monthly splits and guarantees, they still won't do it.

How can they expect to charge that much if they've never paid that much?

You have to understand and appreciate what it's like to invest in something equal to or more expensive than the thing you sell.

**Invest in yourself as you would wish others to invest in you. Only then can you begin to have the right money mindset. You get out what you put in.**

## MISTAKES TO AVOID

- ✗ Charging by the hour.
- ✗ Building before selling.
- ✗ Getting everything 'perfect'.
- ✗ Giving too much information.
- ✗ Focusing on the deliverables rather than the outcome.

## ACTIONS TO TAKE NEXT

- ✓ Brainstorm your niche using the four Ps.
- ✓ Get clear on the six Ps related to your service.
- ✓ Use the marketer's lens to spice up your deliverables.
- ✓ Determine your pricing (please aim higher, as it works).

# Chapter 2
# Message

Your **message** is how you'll distil and convey to your audience the information about you, your service and the outcome.

But if you're anything like me, delaying the work and shiny object syndrome are going to come into play.

I struggled for weeks to come up with a name for what's now called 'Content to Clients'. There was an element of perfectionism for sure, but it was also a case of overthinking it and of not keeping things simple.

I remember stopping outside a Tesco and thinking, *Tesco is such a shit name; what does it even mean?*

Tes. Co.

I'm sure it means something, but as a word, it *means* absolutely nothing. Still, it works because everyone in the UK knows what Tesco is and what it does.

And that's when I thought, *I can let go a bit here.*

The name 'Content to Clients' finally came to me in the shower (the default creative space for entrepreneurs). I didn't overthink it; I'd been doing enough of that already. I'd finally found the name of my programme.

Is it perfect? No.

Does it serve its purpose? Yes. 'Content to Clients' describes the method and the outcome.

It's simple, it's clear and it works.

And that's what matters.

If you're reading this book, it's likely you've got lots of ideas and strong opinions on how you *should* do things. But I guarantee you're already focused on too many things that don't truly matter.

Whilst having ideas and opinions is important, you need to let go of these distractions as they stall action and momentum. They'll always find a way to creep in, and you need to be aware of them and move past them. Fast.

### *Get out of your own way.*

It's easier said than done, but try to let go of your ego and what you *think* people think of you. Whether you're a beginner or not, you have to stop giving a fuck (or stop giving as *much* of a fuck) about how you're perceived.

It'll only slow you down – and we don't have time for that.

## Creating your vision, mission and values

All the gurus and experts out there will tell you that you need to have your **mission, vision** and **values** all nailed down before you start.

Bollocks.

It's just going to get in your way for now.

If you're only at the start of your business journey, how do you know your values? The answer is that you won't until you've actually gone out there and got some experience under your belt.

On the one hand, I do agree that your vision, your mission and your values should inform everything you do, just like your past shapes who you are right now. They should act as a foundational piece of your business:

> **Vision** → Where you're going
>
> **Mission** → How you're going to get there
>
> **Values** → The standards you set for the journey

But if you don't know what these are yet, don't let that get in the way of making progress.

The best way to make progress is to get clients. Doing the work to get people to buy your stuff so you can make it work better.

You might feel the need to skip this bit because it's not obvious straight away, and that's okay. My experience was limited at the start, and I didn't have a strong idea of what my vision, mission and values were. So I pressed the pause button on them.

But now I know C2C works, my vision is bigger, and I can come back to this and work on it. Now I've had time and feedback, these are what ours look like:

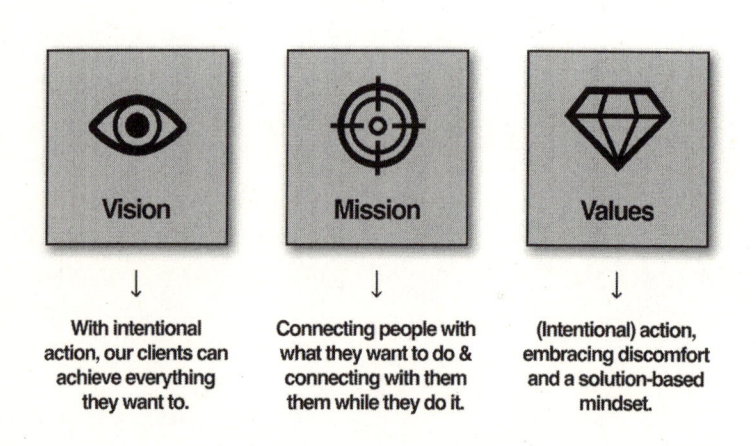

| Vision | Mission | Values |
|---|---|---|
| ↓ | ↓ | ↓ |
| With intentional action, our clients can achieve everything they want to. | Connecting people with what they want to do & connecting with them them while they do it. | (Intentional) action, embracing discomfort and a solution-based mindset. |

This stuff can feel fluffy at the start, so use the simple framework I've just given to figure it out, but do it fast and don't dwell on it too much for now.

Trust that these things will build naturally, rather than forcing them.

# Why do people buy?

### *Even though we're afraid of change, we all want to change something.*

In the last chapter, we explored all the potential problems your clients might be facing and the ways you could help them.

But before you figure out your message, let's take a step back and understand *why* people buy, so you know what they're looking for.

If you think about it, there are obvious and immediate benefits to buying. I call them 'surface-level benefits'. You bought washing-up liquid because you ran out. You bought a takeaway because it's Friday and you can't be bothered to cook.

We think people buy for logical reasons, and they do, but a lot of our logical decisions are *driven* by emotion too.

**People usually buy because it makes them *feel* something.**

Just think about the last few things you've bought.

Maybe you had a bad day at work, so to lift your mood, you bought yourself some chocolate on the way home. On the way home, you remember to go online and buy bedroom curtains because your current ones let in too much light, and you want a good night's sleep. You get home, and the new coat you bought has arrived, so you feel excited because you want to wear it to impress the person you fancy from work. That evening, you go to your PT session because you want to look good and feel healthier. When you get home from your workout, you order a meal delivery, rather than cook, because you feel too tired.

Can you see how we buy things for logical *and* emotional reasons?

We touched on this in the last chapter: the reasons people buy typically fall into three categories:

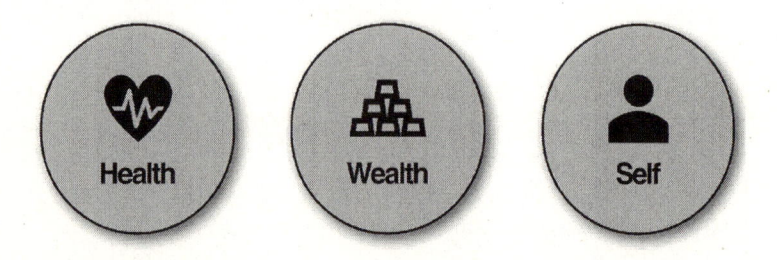

- Health
- Wealth
- Self

Let's take the bedroom curtains you theoretically bought on the way home: you bought them to keep the light out and improve your sleep. That's the surface-level, logical benefit.

But *why* do you want better sleep?

It seems obvious, but dig deeper and think about the long-term reasons. Is it so you can wake up feeling refreshed, have better relationships and have a more chilled-out time at home?

That leads back to **health**, and probably **self** too.

With the coat, you could have just gone and bought one at half the price, but you grabbed a designer one instead.

Why?

The surface-level benefit is that you need a new coat. Simple.

But if you're honest with yourself, it might have been motivated by self. It's a fun and comfy coat. It makes you feel good. And because it's a designer one, it also says something about your status and the image you want to show to the world.

So, let's think about this in terms of business:

| Business | Surface | Deep rooted |
|---|---|---|
| Business coach | More leads, clients | Wealth and/or self |
| Personal trainer | Lose weight | Health and/or self |
| Software provider | Customer service | Wealth |
| Copywriter | Marketing, leads | Wealth |
| Interior designer | Home decor | Self and/or health |
| Videographer | Marketing | Wealth and/or self |

Think about a couple of things you bought recently and answer these two questions:

1. What surface-level benefit did those things provide?
2. What deep-rooted benefit did they offer?

**People will buy from you if you can solve a *deeper-rooted problem* – and lots of these problems are tied to emotions.**

Also, if you can tug on those emotions in your messaging, you'll be the one they turn to for help.

Now you know why people buy, how do we get them to buy from *you?*

## Building a personal brand

Whether you like it or not, you already have a personal brand.

Everyone has one.

And if you want to make more money, I strongly suggest you lean into building yours.

A lot of people get the concept of a brand wrong. They think it's a website, a logo or the fonts you use, but it's none of these.

A brand is a feeling.

**It's the *perception* people have of *the thing.***

**And that thing is you.**

It's like the recipe for a meal. Your personal brand isn't the meal itself but the *ingredients* that work together to create that meal. All that other stuff – the pictures, the fonts and the colours – that's just the garnish on the top.

**Think of it as the way your content, your offer and your message – everything – shape the feelings and associations people have regarding you.**

Take Joe Rogan as an example. The elements that make up his personal brand are things such as his podcasts, comedy, mixed martial arts (MMA) and smoking weed. If you think of Elon Musk, you think of Tesla, Twitter (now X), Space X and loads of money.

With me, hopefully, people think of humour, fitness, actionable content and family. All these things are associated with my brand, and people buy into it because it's relatable and it makes them feel something. But within that, they also see I present an opportunity for them to transform their business by helping them win clients using social media.

### PRO TIP: FACE VS FACELESS

A person is always going to be more relatable to people than a faceless logo.

If you look at Elon Musk's social media accounts versus Tesla's, his following is much, much bigger than his company's.[1,2] If you go to Gary Vaynerchuk's (aka Gary Vee's) personal account and his company's account, he has 10.1m[3] followers compared to his company's, which stands at 253k.[4] Richard Branson has 4.8m[5] compared to Virgin's 241k.[6]

Typically, company pages on LinkedIn and Instagram will have smaller followings than individual accounts. This is because people are less interested in faceless companies.

The following is a concept taken from Russell Brunson, founder of Click Funnels. He says a personal brand can be boiled down to these three things:

## You, mission and opportunity

### 1. You

A personal brand starts with the person. We need to bring *you*, your story and your opinions to the forefront of your marketing.

Who you are will be a massive selling point and a big part of creating your personal brand, so we'll cover this in the next section.

### 2. Mission

Why do you exist? (Aside from making money.)

What impact do you want to make on the world? Do you want to help more women step into leadership roles? Do you want to help more parents find a better work-life balance? Microsoft's mission is to empower every organisation on the planet to achieve more. Apple's is based on user experience.

What's your mission?

**3. Opportunity**

This is what you can do for people.

It's your offer and the transformation or results you create for people, which we worked on in *Chapter 1*.

---

Don't worry if you don't have all three of these things dialled in yet; you'll figure them out. Most people have a good idea of one or two of them, but when you have all three running together, you'll be unstoppable.

No one can question the validity of what you do and who you are.

But at the start, it'll be hard.

No one will know you. You won't have a personal brand to lean on, but by doing the work, creating the content and putting yourself out there, you'll build a brand you can monetise.

People will start getting in touch with you based on the strength of your content. You'll start coming up in conversations. You'll start getting incoming DMs, requests to be on podcasts and enquiries from potential clients.

**You'll become known for what you do.**

Someone joined a sales call with me the other day, and the first thing they said was, 'Oh my God, I feel like I know you.'

**That's what you want your brand to do.**

This is why it's so important: having a *personal* brand is your way of differentiating yourself from the rest of the market. It compounds over time, building 'relationships' in the background as your reputation grows. In turn, people will begin to know, like and trust you.

So put the effort in now to receive gains in the long term.

---

### PRO TIP: SALES IS A PEOPLE-CENTRED BUSINESS

There's a lot of talk about business-to-business (B2B), business-to-consumer (B2C) and direct-to-consumer (D2C) models, but if you look closely, they all have one thing in common: they're all H2H – human to human.

Sales revolves around communication and relationships between *people*. That's why having a *personal* brand is so important.

# Differentiation

There are two types of **differentiation** to understand and use when building a business: personal differentiation and product/offer differentiation.

They both inform and contribute to your personal brand, so keep these in mind as you work through this section.

## Personal differentiation

We're taught from an early age that we're all unique.

But online, most people behave in exactly the same way. They do the same shit, create the same offers, make the same content and do the same pathetic little dance.

That's why they struggle to stand out. They don't communicate what makes them *different*.

And what makes you different is your *story*.

> ***You're your own point of differentiation.***

People *want* connection. They want to feel like they're aligned with the person they're interacting with. They don't want polished perfection; they want raw, authentic, organic and uncut. They want to know you're as flawed, weird and as human as they are. Your audience wants to know *you*. The *real* you.

But a lot of people I speak to think their lives are boring.

They honestly believe they have nothing to add that would make them stand out. But because *they do the same shit all the time, no wonder they think their life's boring.*

However, to the other people watching, it's not boring at all. You can be half a step in front of someone and be their entire inspiration.

***Your story is the most powerful tool you have.***

Your story is how you're going to stand out and attract the right clients for your business.

So how do you get that across? Take a look at this list, as these things are what make you different and make you exciting:

- Relationships
- Appearance
- Background
- Insecurities
- Upbringing
- Worldview
- Successes
- Opinions
- Location
- Hobbies
- Journey
- Childhood
- Failures
- Quirks
- Career
- Beliefs
- House
- Values
- Loves
- Hates
- Diet
- Pets

As clichéd as it sounds, it's about well and truly being yourself. Use this list to write down some things about yourself and to start getting clear on your story. Ask yourself questions such as these:

- → What do you love? And hate?
- → What have you succeeded at?
- → What have you failed miserably at?
- → What strong opinions do you have?
- → Where have you lived and where do you live now? Why?

> The things that make you different are your unfair advantage. And *everyone* has one.
>
> It's the things that you take for granted and that seem unimportant and unremarkable. Those are what will make you stand out.

I once had a guy on a call who wanted to sell leadership development coaching.

'What did you do before this?' I asked him.

'I used to be the headmaster of a high school,' he said.

That got my interest. I found out that he only got two GCSEs, and that's when I told him, 'That's your angle. That's your hook.' From two GCSEs to headmaster to leadership coach. What's not compelling about that? His past story is the unfair advantage that'll make him stand out.

*But I don't want to be myself online,* you might think.

How many other people are feeling like that? There will be people throughout the world who will feel the same as you and will *want* what you sell or will benefit from seeing your content.

**You owe it to them to show up and demonstrate what's possible.**

Sharing your story doesn't necessarily mean going all the way back to when you were born.

**Don't share anything you're not comfortable with.**

It's about sharing enough of yourself that people can start to know you, like you and trust you.

Take a moment to think about it:

- → What experience, skill or knowledge do you have that makes you different?
- → What's your unfair advantage (that you probably think is boring)?
- → What puts you just half a step in front of someone else?
- → What could you teach someone?

This is where the argument for having a personal brand comes in: *it communicates your point of differentiation.*

And that's what's going to bring you attention, leads and, eventually, clients.

## Product/offer differentiation

There's a concept used by massive companies to differentiate themselves from their competitors. It's called the blue ocean strategy (and the book of the same name is great, by the way),[7] and it's a useful way to position your offer in the market:

Imagine a red ocean and a blue ocean. In the red ocean, the waters are bloody because the people in your space all look and sound the same – and they're fighting each other for a bite of fresh meat. They're competing with everyone else, and a lot of the time, they're forced to compromise on either quality, price or both. They can't charge what they want because the price is dictated by the people buying.

But in the blue ocean, there's only one shark.

**And it's you.**

The waters are nice and clear; there's no blood. You have no competitors, so you can create a brand-new demand for your service. Theoretically, you can charge whatever the hell you want because there's no one else doing anything like you.

Take Amazon, Uber and Airbnb: they all operate within a blue ocean. They don't have any direct competitors that come anywhere close to them, and they obliterated the competition by being so different that no one else could compete.

Your point of difference doesn't just have to be about you personally, either. It can be found within the offer, the service, the customer journey or another part of the business.

But they're big companies, and you're just a person, so how can you do it?

- → The name of your business could be so unusual or fun that people rethink your industry.
- → You could show up on your socials in a way that isn't normally associated with your niche.
- → The parts of your offer could be streamlined, personalised, automated or done in person.
- → Your response time could be 24 hours rather than three days.
- → The community part of your offer could be face to face, rather than in a Facebook group.
- → You donate a percentage of your profit to a charitable cause.
- → You offer in-person, one-to-one coaching in their home for convenience.
- → You have an app.

The possibilities are endless.

What can you do, talk about, create or offer that no one else in your space is doing?

## Simplicity

At this stage, you'll probably have so many ideas that you're going to overcomplicate things. You'll want to have everything ready now, and it's not going to be.

The good news is that you don't have to, and probably never will, have everything – or anything – fully worked out.

You'll constantly refine and improve it, so you might as well throw your hat in the ring and commit to action – now!

You don't need to build a website. You don't need to spend two days strategising. You don't need to know your vision, mission and values. You don't need printed T-shirts or coasters with the logo on them. You don't need a neon sign in your office.

**No T-shirts**     **No neon signs**     **No website**

**These things do not serve you. They're distractions.**

I'm speaking from experience here because I used to be that person. I spent too long on too many things that didn't matter. You can call it perfectionism or procrastination, but neither of them are your friend.

What you need to do now is take your offer and your top-level message out to market, and then see what works.

In order to keep it simple, just remind yourself of this:

- → Who do you help?
- → What do you help them achieve?
- → How do you help them achieve it?
- → How quickly can you help them achieve it?
- → What is and isn't included?

Don't come and tell me you've made a brilliant website and printed out your business cards. Quite frankly, I don't give a fuck. And neither should you.

How much money have you made?

Go out and have conversations with people and start getting some traction. And to do that, you're going to want to read the next chapter.

## MISTAKES TO AVOID

- ✗ Hiding behind a logo.
- ✗ Creating the same things as other people.
- ✗ Obsessing over your mission, vision and values.
- ✗ Self-censorship and not putting the real you out there.
- ✗ Building a website or something else you don't need yet.

## ACTIONS TO TAKE NEXT

- ✓ Write down your mission, vision and values (fast).
- ✓ What makes you different? Use the list in this chapter to prompt you.
- ✓ List some potential personal/product points of differentiation.
- ✓ Brainstorm surface-level and logical reasons why people would buy from you. And then do the same for the deep-rooted, emotional reasons.

# ⚠ WARNING!

You need to get this into your head as fast as possible:

**You're reading this book because you want to grow. You want to grow your business, the number of leads and the number of clients. You want more money. You want more security and success.**

In the coming chapters, I'm going to show you how to do that, but...

If you focus on *anything* other than selling, growth won't happen. You now know what makes a good offer and how to position yourself.

Anything you do from this point on, other than creating sales opportunities, is just a distraction.

You can't grow inside your comfort zone.

So make a choice now and commit to it.

**I'll repeat this once more: if you focus on *anything* other than selling, you're stalling your progress.**

*There is no downside to doing this work. Absolutely none.*

# Chapter 3
# Traction

My wife Amy used to sell health and beauty products for a multi-level marketing (MLM) company. She had to sell weight-loss products, hand gels, creams, lotions and potions – that kind of thing. The goal was to recruit other people to work underneath her, and then she'd get a percentage of the money they made.

(Yes, it's basically a pyramid scheme!)

Amy's very switched on and personable, and academically, she's very clever.

But she didn't find much success with her new side hustle.

And I think the reason is that the cleverer people are and the more switched on they are, the more they intellectualise, internalise, and…

… **overthink.**

She initially found success using her existing network; she sold to her family and a few friends. But when it came to speaking to strangers and publishing content online (which I did try to help with), she ended up overthinking and analysis paralysis kicked in.

She wasn't making any sales, and it began to feed her negative thought patterns.

In reality, she *wasn't putting in the effort* required to achieve any sales.

I see this a lot with coaches and freelancers. They'll quit their nine-to-five and speak to old friends, ex-employers, ex-colleagues and family. They'll make a few sales and think, *This is going brilliantly; this is going great. I can do this. It's easy!*

They've got that 'uninformed optimism'.

But when their existing network is squeezed dry and they realise they don't have anything sustainable, they begin to think it's impossible. They start to tell themselves that story of 'Oh, I can't do this. I mustn't be any good at it.'

They start having thoughts and seeing patterns that back up their negative beliefs, even if it's not true. That then gets fed through to their actions.

And that creates their negative reality.

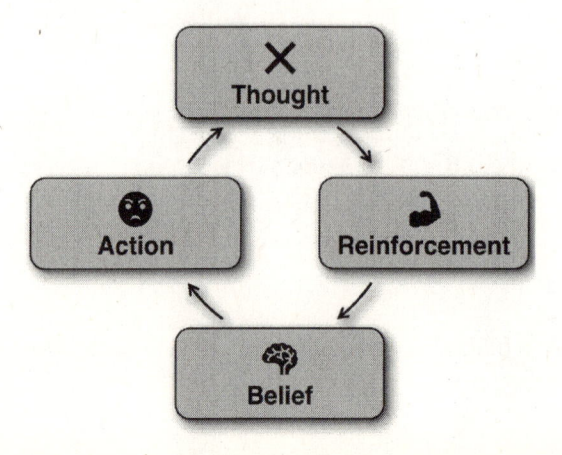

**If you're incapable of breaking your limiting beliefs, your thoughts will become your reality, and you'll fail.**

However, it doesn't have to be like that.

'The magic you're looking for is in the work you're avoiding.' I don't know who said this (and neither does the internet, apparently!), but it's absolutely spot on. Confront the work, because leads aren't going to jump out at you.

**You need to go to *them*.**

And that's what this chapter is going to help you achieve.

When building **traction**, your goal is this:

**Don't focus on anything other than having conversations and communicating your offer.**

Who do you help? How do you help them?

Shout it from the rooftops, if you have to.

Having conversations with people and continuing that conversation to the point of working with clients (for free or for money) or to the point of a referral is all that matters in this exercise. (It matters in business too, but for this chapter, our goal is to just get your business moving.)

You'll need to advance with speed and resilience for this to work. Now is *not* the time to overthink.

### *Make the decision to build traction now.*

Before I started my business, I wanted to make content and put it out there for about five years, but I didn't have the balls to do it. I let that decision and those negative thought patterns weigh on me and delay my progress.

**The longer you leave a decision unmade, the more energy it drains from you.**

Think of your decision-making like a battery: when you wake up, it's at 100%.

Every decision you *avoid* making, you *can't make quickly* or you *overanalyse*, brings that energy bar down.

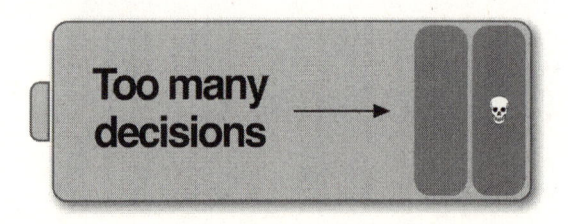

**Act now, before your battery runs out.**

And I know what you're thinking:

*But this is* supposed *to be hard.*

Lots of people who are in the early stages of running a business will find any excuse to avoid doing the hard work.

I know this because I've done it myself.

You'll want to go off and build a lead magnet first, worry about your engagement rate, or set up a separate Instagram page for your business.

**Stop. You do not need any of these things. Seriously.**

*Nothing else matters other than starting conversations and booking calls.*

And it doesn't matter if your offer isn't fully built.

At this stage, it probably shouldn't be – yet. But that's okay.

Doing this traction work is going to give you these:

- ✓ Experience in *articulating* your offer
- ✓ Experience in *delivering* your offer
- ✓ Feedback for *improving* your offer

You'll find out whether what you've put together is viable and sellable and whether it's good enough that you don't need to make any major changes to it.

But that isn't the only outcome.

There are a few more you'll experience when you do this traction work well:

**Clients**: People will like your offer and want to pay you.

- → This will lead to money and more experience.

**Referrals**: People will know others who might be interested.

- → This will lead to more conversations and more leads.

**Social proof** (either from working for free or paid): You'll get testimonials, screenshots and reviews.

- → This will build your library of marketing assets.

**Feedback:** People will give you their opinions to optimise your offer.

- → This will lead to an improved offer.

**Free clients** (optional)**:** People will let you use them as a test for free.

- → This will lead to more experience, feedback and social proof.

*Now is the time to put away the notes and get your hands dirty.*

Doing this work is going to require a lot from you. It's going to feel overwhelming, and you should expect that. Of course, you're going to feel insecure. Remember, this isn't *supposed* to be easy.

You're going to have to be comfortable stepping out of your comfort zone and living in that area of *dis*comfort.

I view entrepreneurship as a never-finished, never-ending jigsaw: nothing ever feels done. The minute you find the right piece, another gap will appear, and you'll have to go and find a piece for that one. A lot of the time, there'll be 10 pieces missing, so that feeling of insecurity and discomfort is absolutely normal.

**But I promise you there's no downside to doing this work. Absolutely none.**

Your mission here is to speak to people consistently. I'm going to show you how to go out into the market, into every avenue and into every channel that you can possibly think of. And I'll tell you how to have conversations with as many people as you can about your offer.

There are five phases to go through to create traction:

1. Determining **who** to contact.
2. Determining **how** to contact them.
3. Determining **when** to contact them.
4. Determining **what** to say.
5. Having **the traction conversation**.

***When you step out of your comfort zone, you grow.***

## Who to contact

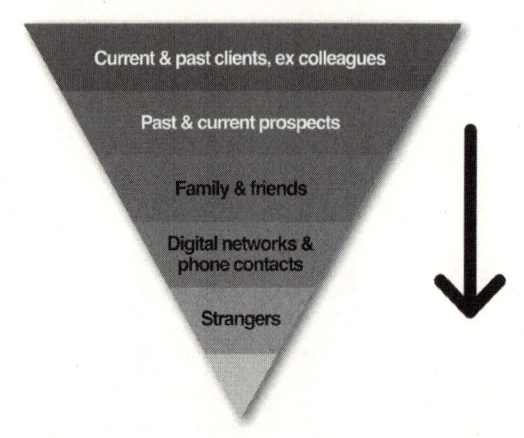

- Current & past clients, ex colleagues
- Past & current prospects
- Family & friends
- Digital networks & phone contacts
- Strangers

There are a few different people and methods you can use in order to start reaching out to people, and I've organised these into five levels.

*Level 1. Current clients, past clients and ex-colleagues*

These will be your current clients (paid or free) if you have any, past clients, ex-colleagues and other contacts in your industry.

*Level 2. Past and current prospects*

These will be people you've had a few conversations with but who haven't converted, for whatever reason; leads that you're nurturing right now; or people who've have booked calls with you in the past (even if they don't feel particularly relevant to your new offer).

*Level 3. Family and friends*

This isn't about getting hired by your little brother. This is about getting connected to *his* network.

Think about how many people your *family* are connected to and how many people *they* know who have lives and jobs that need help. Even your grandma knows people you don't know.

Alongside this, speaking to your family and friends is going to inform them that you're working on something new. This might not pay off straight away, but your efforts in building a new business or working on a new project will spark interest (and, hopefully, support).

*Level 4. Digital networks and phone contacts*

Every single person reading this book probably has a social media account with at least 500 friends, followers or connections. Think about those.

Also think about the people in your phone's contacts list, the people you meet on nights out, friends of friends, taxi drivers, school teachers, mums from school, dads from school and the football group – whatever it may be.

What WhatsApp groups or Facebook community groups are you in? What about people you've met via online events? Anyone you're connected to digitally should be on your list.

*Level 5. Strangers*

Recently, I was at one of my daughter's martial arts classes and I overheard another parent speaking on the phone about Instagram. So I asked her, 'How's Instagram going?'

She said, 'I'm really shit at it.'

And we ended up having a conversation. She wasn't the right person for me to help, but we're now in contact, and she's aware I help people with social media. Do *not* rule out strangers.

---

### PRO TIP: START WARM

When you start reaching out, you'll find that the warmer the relationship, the easier the conversation. Level 1, 2 and 3 people will be the easiest to approach and talk to.

But that doesn't mean you shouldn't try level 4 and 5 people.

You may have picked this book up because you're focused on social media, but that doesn't mean your communication should be limited to online only.

You never know what people are looking for, so go further…

---

***Opportunity is everywhere, and there's no downside to having a conversation with anyone and everyone.***

Remember, all we want are conversations, introductions and feedback.

There have been people who've come into C2C and landed clients in 48 hours by utilising their little black book, going through their offer at a top level and having a couple of conversations.

It *is* possible.

Now grab a pen and paper or your favourite note-taking app, and then make a list of *everyone* you could speak to:

- → Your email contacts
- → Your client database/list
- → People you see on the school run
- → Any forums you're involved with
- → Your whole list of phone contacts
- → Your WhatsApp group conversations
- → The saleswoman who sold you your car
- → Your window cleaner, your gardener, etc.
- → Every social media platform you have access to
- → People you know who are well connected / rich
- → People you know who are established in business
- → The electrician you know who did some work on a famous person's mansion
- → Any communities you're a part of, either online or in person (your kids' sports clubs, chess club from 1972, PTA, etc.)

**Can you see how *massive* your extended network is?**

You only need one person to introduce you to their cousin's girlfriend's best friend's barber, and you could have your first client. So go out there and start speaking to as many people as possible, as fast as possible.

> ### PRO TIP: WHERE ELSE TO FIND PROSPECTS
>
> - Exhibitions
> - Communities
> - Co-working spaces
> - Relevant audio or live events
> - Referrals (we'll touch on this later)
> - Chamber of Commerce / governing bodies
> - Guest training in other people's communities
> - People from associated or overlapping industries
> - In your local area, businesses networking groups and the press

## How to contact people

Now you know who to contact, how do you do it?

When my friends are trying to organise a night out, someone will put together a WhatsApp group. They'll add 30 people in there and then ask a question.

Only about 15 will respond.

Others won't respond at all.

And some will leave without saying a thing.

Those people who don't respond don't necessarily feel the need to (and it's easier to hide behind so many other people). But if you send them a DM and say, 'Hey, Dave, are you free on the 30th to go out for a few beers?' Dave will respond because it's just you and him. And that's human nature. We respond better to a more personalised message.

It's a direct versus an indirect way of communicating, and you'll want to use both for the best outcomes. The direct way is known as the one-to-one method, and the indirect way is the one-to-many method.

## One-to-one

One-to-one methods of communication include:

- Face to face
- Phone call (warm/cold)
- Direct text, DM or email (warm/cold)

When you speak to people one-to-one, you're much more likely to get a response.

But if you're not confident speaking to people directly, this could feel difficult. Using this method long term also takes a lot of effort. There's no leverage or scalability. You'll only be able to communicate with one person at a time, so if you don't have a sales team or virtual assistant (VA), this method won't be sustainable. You'll need to combine it with one-to-many.

## One-to-many

One-to-many methods of communication include:

- Posting content (we'll cover this later)
- Emails (warm/cold)
- Lives/masterclasses
- Communities
- Group chats

One-to-many communication is very easy to do. You publish something once, and it goes to lots of people. But even though you can reach 10k people through your content, your messaging will be a lot broader and less specific, and the response rate will probably be much lower than one-to-one.

There are no prizes for guessing which is the preferred and more effective method; building an audience to speak to one-to-many gives you the ultimate leverage. But don't rule out one-to-one either. We're going to use it a lot in this chapter.

## When to contact people

Now you know the **who** and **how**, it's time for the **when**.

And you know what I'm going to say: it's *now*.

The longer you wait, the harder this gets. It's as simple as that.

In terms of decision-making, the longer you wait, the less money you make. If you sit and let it marinate, procrastinate, and overthink this shit, you're going to fail. Or at least you'll have very, very slow progress.

The time to start is *now*.

> ***You* learn *through action,*** 
> ***not planning and strategy.***

I took action and went out to market – with the wrong offer; I tried to build a one-to-many solution on Instagram.

But it was through taking that action that I learned I didn't have enough eyeballs. I had 1,500 followers and not enough attention. But I also got to test my offer and speak to people in the market who gave me advice. It was through doing so that I was able to create what would become C2C.

I learned some key lessons in real time by going out with the minimum viable product – and so can you.

**The time to do this is now.**

The whole beauty of this traction exercise is that you can do it anytime. Don't just do this once and forget about it. Consistently think of new and existing places you can go, start conversations and draw attention to your offer.

## What to say

Simply put, you want to tell people quickly you'd like to speak to them:

- → To gather their thoughts and get feedback
- → To arrange a Zoom call / meeting for a longer chat

There are two types of people you're going to approach: people you know and people you don't. And you'll need to communicate with them in slightly different ways. Use the following templates as a guide.

BUILD · CHAPTER 3 - TRACTION | 91

## PRO TIP: BE *NORMAL*

You don't have to apply pressure or make yourself feel sleazy, you're just asking people if they want to have a conversation. You're not trying to sell them anything; you only want some feedback or a couple of introductions. Don't overthink this and turn it into something it's not.

## Templates

***For the people you know (one-to-one via DMs, calls, emails or face to face)***

Alter this according to your situation and the relationship you have with the person. Don't overwhelm them when you first start. Personalise it and use words that sound like you.

> Hey *[name]*, been a while…
>
> How's *[common interest / new thing / family / spouse / job]* going…?
>
> I've just put together this new *[thing / business / package]* and I'd love to get your feedback on it.
>
> Are you free for a quick Zoom? How's *[tomorrow afternoon]*?

**Chris James**

Founder @
Content To Clients

If you're speaking face to face, you might run them through your offer there and then. If it's over text or DM, it might take a few messages.

***For the people you don't know (one-to-one via DMs, calls and emails)***

> Hey *[name]*, we've not spoken before, but I was hoping you could help me:

> I *[can see / love the fact that you're] [doing something new / fun / exciting]*. *[Potentially ask how the thing is going]*.

> I'm looking for 3 *[target audience]* who want to *[outcome]*. *[Completely free of charge]*. Do you know anyone?

> I've *[insert relevant experience]* & think *[you could benefit / it's worth a conversation]*. *[Consider adding any social proof / results]*. Are you free for a Zoom on [Tuesday] ?

Again, alter this according to the situation, the person and how you naturally communicate. Add or remove bits as necessary.

## The traction conversation

Okay, so now you've gone through your lists and gone absolutely nuts taking action every single day, you'll hopefully have some calls or some meetings in the diary.

That's amazing, but what are you going to say on the call?

> ## PRO TIP: MINDSET
>
> Don't overthink or overhype it in your brain. We're not pitching here; we're not selling.
>
> **This isn't a sales call.**
>
> This is just a conversation about this new project/business/idea you have. And all you're trying to do is get referrals or some feedback. If the person you're speaking to is a good fit, they'll let you know, and that's when you sell to them.
>
> But try to enter into these exchanges with no expectations.

The context of your conversations will depend on whether you think this person is close to your target market or not.

## Not close to the target market

If they're not close to your target market (e.g. you're an accountant, but they have a full-time job and therefore are unlikely to need one) and you're 100% confident you can't sell to them, you'll want to run through your offer at a very high level.

Get their feedback on the price, the duration, the promise and the phases.

What sounds good? What doesn't sound good? Is it too cheap? Does it sound like it takes too long? What doesn't make sense? Is there anything else you think I could add? Get as much info as you can.

And then towards the end of that, you can say this:

'I appreciate you hearing me out. Will you do me a massive favour and introduce me to two or three people you think this might be relevant to? If they sign up, I'm happy to give you a kickback [or some other offer you're comfortable with].'

It'll sound forward, and it might be a bit uncomfortable, but all you need to do is ask them to do it immediately, and it's unlikely they'll say no.

## Close to the target market

If they *are* in your target market, or close to it, you want to be a little bit more strategic.

You'll want to find out more about *their* situation:

- → What are they doing at the moment?
- → What problems keep cropping up?
- → What's stopping them from achieving what they want?
- → How long have they been involved in this?
- → Where do they want to get to?

- → Why haven't they been able to get there yet?
- → What have they tried that hasn't worked?
- → And hypothetically speaking, if you put together a process or an offer that completely guarantees to solve the problems they've mentioned, how much would they pay for it? They'll tell you a price, and then you can run through the offer (again, hypothetically) and ask for feedback and referrals.

If the person you're speaking to is interested, they may come out and say, 'Actually, this sounds like something I need help with,' which is the perfect outcome.

You then have a decision to make: you either pitch them or offer a free trial in return for a testimonial. (Personally, I'd take the money.)

### PRO TIP: RESEARCH

Make sure you keep track of all your research and findings as you have these conversations. What kind of feedback do you keep getting?

If the same positive comments keep cropping up, you're on to a winner.

If only negative comments crop up, you might want to change the element of the offer they relate to.

## Referrals

The best introductions you can get will involve the person who's doing the introduction. So, rather than just getting a name or a number, if possible, get the introducer to remain *inside* the conversation.

For example, the introducer sends an email or starts a group chat with you and the person they're introducing.

Why?

Because the referee will be more inclined to respond if the person they know is still in the conversation.

Hopefully, the people you end up being introduced to will be even closer to your target market.

Get them on a call and repeat the process so they either buy or introduce you further. You can learn a lot more about selling on calls in the last third of this book.

## Preparation is key

Not everyone is going to respond positively to this, so brace yourself.

But don't get disheartened.

Now here's the harsh reality: *you aren't entitled to incoming opportunities.*

This is a volume game, so you need to put out activity and messages on a *massive* scale. We still send up to 100 DMs a day. If we send 100 messages a day, over the course of four weeks, that's 2k messages. If a (half-established) business like us is doing 2k messages a month, you – as a new and growing business looking to get traction – should probably be doing even more.

That's why you need to make sure you've got time carved out in the diary for this. If you don't, you'll stay stuck.

**And I know you've not bought this book because you *want* to stay stagnant and spinning your tyres…**

I'm sure you've heard of MrBeast, but if not, check him out on YouTube.[8] What most people don't know is that he started in 2012. In the beginning, he had about five years of getting no traction whatsoever on the platform, consistently publishing content, consistently pushing his message out there and getting low money, low views and low numbers of subscribers.

But then something happened in 2018. All of a sudden, his number of subscribers took off. If you graphed it, it would look like a massive hockey stick. That's the result of all the traction he had been building. He finally hit a point and then, *boom*, momentum propelled him upwards. There was a massive spike in growth.

That's his non-stop effort, work, blood, sweat and tears compounding over time. By 2022, he had over 90 million subscribers.

At the time of writing this book, he has amassed 6 million subscribers in the last 30 days, but no one cared for five fucking years!

**Overnight success takes time (years in some cases), so have a bit of self-belief and do the work now.**

Here's a great joke I heard recently:

'You believed in Santa Claus for 10 years; you can believe in yourself for five minutes.'

> ### PRO TIP: ALWAYS BE OPEN TO REFERRALS
>
> Never, ever, ever stop looking for introductions or referrals.
>
> Companies pay thousands to acquire customers through paid advertising, but you can do it simply by sending a few messages and making a few phone calls.
>
> It's the cheapest and the easiest way to build traction.

## MISTAKES TO AVOID

- ✗ Making excuses.
- ✗ Saying, 'I don't know anyone.'
- ✗ Holding back from publishing content.
- ✗ Being afraid of the word 'no'. You're going to hear it a lot.

## ACTIONS TO TAKE NEXT

- ✓ Decide who you'll contact (levels 1–5).
- ✓ List the one-to-one methods you'll use.
- ✓ Prepare what you're going to write/say in your messages.
- ✓ Block out time in your calendar to start contacting people.
- ✓ Book those calls, be normal and show up to help, not to sell.
- ✓ Be ready to learn about the one-to-many method in *Chapter 5*.

# Offer-Building Blueprint

**Free Download**

Download your free offer-building blueprint by scanning the following QR code:

Or by visiting chris-james.co/book-obb

# MARKET 2

*If your clients are in Egypt, don't piss about in France*

# Chapter 4
# Journey

When I started in sales, I didn't know what the fuck I was getting into.

On our first day, me and another acne-ridden new-starter were sitting in a room with a bunch of other naïve amateurs – and were thrown into hell.

I'll never forget it: my new team leader, Max, ripped a 400+ page *Yellow Pages* in half and gave me the A's to L's, and gave the M's to Z's to the other guy. We were given a script, told briefly what we were selling and instructed to make 220 cold calls a day, with our only training being the people sitting near us.

**I absolutely hated it.**

But I'm glad I had the experience. When you have to make 200+ cold calls a day – with *timed* toilet breaks – you don't have time to let fear take over.

(Even though, sometimes, I'd just ring and leave a lengthy silent voicemail simply to make my call time appear higher.)

Taking action, gathering data and getting experience is what truly helped me to improve in sales.

One thing I discovered after doing hundreds of cold calls was that I only had about 15 seconds before the person on the other end zoned out and put the phone down.

**Only 15 seconds to gain their trust. Maybe less.**

They didn't know me. They weren't expecting to hear from me. They didn't trust me. Why should they?

Pitching to prospects as soon as they answered was never going to work for me, so I had to show them I wasn't one of *those* guys. I was there to make them like me, not piss them off.

So, I put in the effort to sound different to every other cold-caller.

Every word in that first conversation, and in the conversations after that, was positioned for that exact outcome. (Even if it took me years to actually get good).

Because every touchpoint is a journey in showing your clients that you're different and you can be trusted.

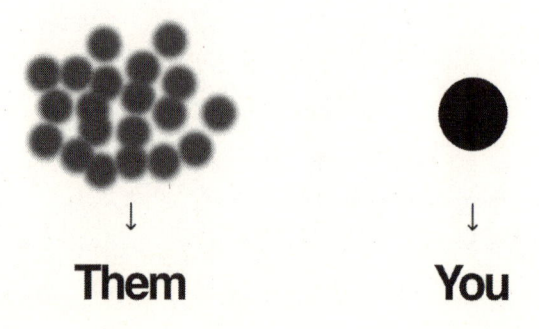

↓ ↓

**Them**     **You**

## Everything is a journey

Building 'know, like and trust' with potential clients is a crucial part of business, and to do that we have to take them on a journey.

But this is the step a lot of people are inclined to skip or cut corners on, because, if we're honest with ourselves, we're all inherently lazy.

We want everything quickly.

We'd all rather go to the gym and have a six-pack on day two than put in months of work. Most people don't want to go through the sweat or discomfort required to reach the end goal…

… and that's why most people get shit results.

When we're lazy, we leave loose ends and make mistakes like these:

- → A potential client downloads a lead magnet, but there's no call to action (CTA) to tell them where to go next, so they drop off the radar.
- → A prospect books a call, but there's no process to strengthen the relationship between the call being booked and the call taking place, so the conversation starts on the wrong foot.
- → Content isn't planned in advance, so the marketing is last minute, reactive and, ultimately, confusing.

**These loose ends are why content, products and ideas flop.**

Taking people from stranger to client in two seconds flat is the wrong approach. It's like trying to *teleport* from England to Dubai when, in fact, there are many, many stages you have to go through in order to travel to that destination.

Try to keep a zoomed-out perspective of your *entire* customer journey. Understand each step they need to take and how those steps contribute to the client reaching their destination.

> ### PRO TIP: MICRO-CONVERSIONS
>
> Within every client journey, there will also be a number of smaller journeys too. In sales and marketing, they're called 'micro-conversions' or 'micro-journeys'.
>
> These are just as important as the main one, so be just as aware of these.

When business owners or marketing teams begin planning the customer journey, they often begin with the start in mind.

But that's the reason they fail.

**You need to start with the *end* in mind.**

I've got no doubt that C2C works so well because it's reverse-engineered from very specific end goals. From a delivery standpoint and a marketing standpoint, most of what we do is engineered backwards from our objective.

For example, when we're trying to push prospects into a sales call, we're very intentional about how we get them there. We know what happens right before a call, two steps before that and all the way back to that first contact.

That's why it's important to focus on the end first: what's your ultimate objective?

If it's to get people on a call, how can you make that journey as smooth as possible? Ask yourself these questions:

- → What instructions do they need?
- → What signposts or signals will help?
- → What do you need to make people feel?
- → What do you need to make people think?
- → How can you make it easier or simpler for them?

*Everything* in your marketing should be intentional, so the journey should be *engineered* to get the outcome you want.

## Choosing your channels

The first thing to do when engineering your journey is to choose the right channels.

You should have already done a lot of the groundwork for this in *Chapter 1. Offer*, which is to understand exactly who your audience are, what they're struggling with and where they want to get to.

When you know that, you'll be able to meet them where they are – *literally*.

For example, if your objective is to sell to high-level CEOs, they're not all going to be hanging around on social media. If you're selling to teenagers, there's a good chance (at the time this book was written) they're on TikTok or Snapchat. If you're selling to people who are professionals, LinkedIn is probably the right place to go.

Your clients might listen to podcasts or prefer in-person networking events. They might travel constantly, so billboards, magazines or even radio might be the best choice. It might be sending a copy of your new book to their office, just so they know who you are.

**Understanding where your audience actually spends their time is important.**

**If your clients are in Egypt**
↓

**Don't piss about in France**
↓

So, the best place to position yourself is where your prospects spend the most time and where you can gain the most exposure to them. Make some notes on where your audience likes to hang out. If they hang out in lots of different places, pick the most popular, but in line with how easily you can reach them there too.

If you're unsure about where they hang out, either ask your existing clients or someone in the industry/space you're targeting.

Here's a story. I don't know if it's true, but it's fucking brilliant.

Company A was trying to sell to CEO B, so they figured out the route he drove to work each day and bought advertising space on *every single billboard* on that route. All to get his attention and, ultimately, his business.

**That's the level of commitment you want to aspire to. Occupy the space you know your target audience is going to be in and put up as many metaphorical billboards as you can.**

This might all seem obvious, but you'd be surprised by how many people's businesses stagnate because they *aren't* willing to be uncomfortable and occupy a space that their clients operate in.

To them, I'd say this:

**Your addiction to comfort is costing you money.**

This isn't about spamming people or being annoying, it's about meeting your potential clients where *they* are most comfortable. And if that means learning how to use LinkedIn or Instagram, that's what you have to do.

> **PRO TIP: MINDSET**
>
> None of this is about you.
>
> This is about your client and what they need to achieve a transformation. If you aren't meeting them where they are, they're never going to see your potential – or even see you, for that matter.

Once you've chosen your channel(s), it's not enough to hang around and hope for the best; it's time to think about all the different touchpoints you can maximise.

## The seven billboards

A touchpoint is any form of interaction between you and your potential client.

Imagine it as one of those metaphorical billboards on your client's route to their destination. It's an advert, a website, a live chat, a company event, a point of sale, a shopfront, a newsletter, a loyalty card, a purchase confirmation email, a video tutorial, a testimonial, a book… You get the idea.

> For the purpose of *this* book, we're going to talk about **content** touchpoints. But if other types are relevant to your business, it's worth spending time exploring those options too.

There's an unwritten law in marketing (I can't be sure, as the numbers are never really exact) that says people need about seven points of contact, seven hours or seven 'exposures' to you, your business, or your service before they act.

Think back to the last four-figure purchase you made. Maybe it was for furniture, designer clothes or a holiday. You probably had several, maybe more, touchpoints before you felt ready to buy.

My last big purchase was a $15k mastermind, and I'd been following the guy for over a year. Think of all the videos, emails and posts I'd consumed before taking the leap and booking a call!

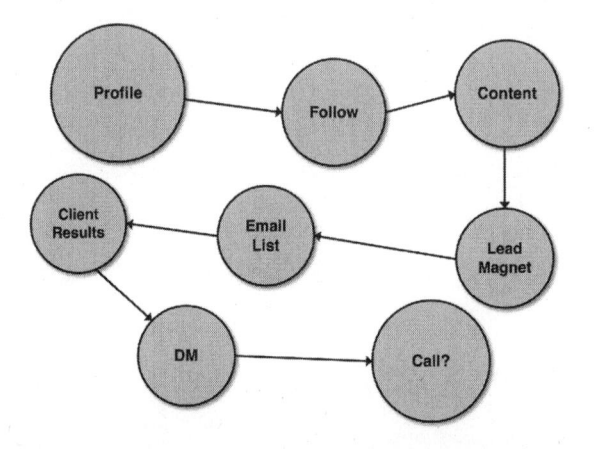

The best strategy is to have content touchpoints in *different* mediums, which is what we're going to talk about in the next chapter.

I've found that having *different formats* and *different placements* ensure that my brand feels like it's everywhere, even if it's just on one or two platforms.

Here are some examples of content touchpoints:

- A DM
- A video
- An email
- A blog post
- A comment
- A lead magnet

This is a journey that should be engineered at a granular level to ensure your potential clients end up at the right destination.

Now not everyone who sees your stuff is going to become a client, but the most important thing is that the journey is put together to take the *right* people – your *ideal* client – from stranger to raving fan.

I appreciate that, early in your journey, you're probably not going to want to go in too deep. However, there are certain things you should have in place when you think about your potential touchpoints.

If we use the earlier story, you've got to make sure each billboard or touchpoint is optimised for that specific part of the journey. They need to flow in a logical, sequential order and be designed in a way to make people *want* to keep moving towards the next one.

From a zoomed-out perspective, think of it like this:

→ The profile sells the follow
→ The follow shows the content

- → The content builds familiarity
- → The familiarity builds the trust
- → The trust builds the conversion

Every touchpoint needs to keep moving people forwards to the next one.

And they don't just need to be in different formats. They need to cover different topics and different angles and to hit people from different emotional and logical standpoints too. We'll talk about these in the next chapter.

Another thing we'll talk about in the next chapter is my CTC method. This keeps things beautifully simple.

I want to show it to you right now:

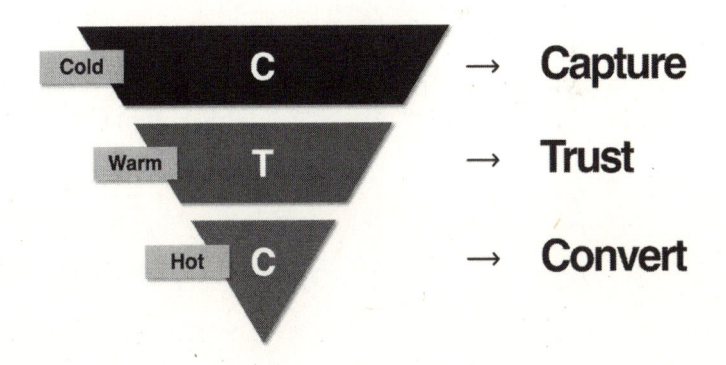

Cold C → **Capture**

Warm T → **Trust**

Hot C → **Convert**

This is the journey (or the 'funnel') in its simplest form: taking people from cold to hot.

Easy, right?

**No. A lot needs to happen on a customer's journey, and in reality, a customer's journey is a lot more complicated.**

It might take some prospects longer than others to travel from one billboard to the next. They might get distracted and veer off down a country lane, some might hit a pothole and have to turn around, and some might go right back to the first one.

You're building a personal brand. You need to engineer this journey to make sure your potential clients have enough exposure to your brand, your intent and yourself that they *want* to act. If they veer off course for any reason, you have ways of redirecting them back to the main road.

**Different touchpoints will lead to different destinations.**

And those destinations don't just have to be actions. They can be thoughts or emotions, but for the most part, they should all help your client to solve part of their problem. This is why having a clear objective and message helps when you engineer the journey.

## The journey overview

At the start, your objective should be to bring eyeballs to your content or your profile. It should have a crystal-clear message that'll attract the right audience so they'll want to go on this journey with you.

In our programme, we teach four key daily activities that activate the different parts of the CTC method. I've called it the '4C workflow', and it's this:

1. Posting a piece of **content**.
2. Interacting with specific accounts/players in your space via making **comments**.
3. **Connecting** with, or following, 20 new people a day.
4. Starting/continuing **conversations** or DM exchanges.

(You'll learn more about these activities in *Chapter 6*.)

There are other things you can do, but generally, the first thing should be getting eyeballs on your content and on your profile.

Once you've got *consistent* attention (and hopefully, your first few clients), you can make the shift to the next stage in *your* journey: **inbound activity**.

You'll start getting new followers, likes and views. It's at this point in the journey that I recommend giving people things that are going to keep them engaged: standout lead magnets, video sales letters and sales assets with dialled-in CTAs. Alongside being very, very responsive to any DMs you receive or maybe some low-level email automation to communicate off platform.

This is where you drive your prospects forwards. You show them what's coming and prove why they need to stay on this path with you.

**Remember to keep the journey easy, engaging and consistent.**

Don't keep clients moving for five billboards and then make them drive another 700 miles to the next one when they're *finally* interested.

## Strike whilst they're hot

A massive mistake that loads of people make is to not capitalise on the prospect when they're at their absolute hottest.

Let's say, I've just booked a sales call with you, but there's a three-day gap between now and the date we've agreed to talk.

Are you nurturing the relationship in that gap? Are you strengthening the perception of how amazing you are by providing links to testimonials, explainer videos or social proof? If not…

It's like getting people to drive past that fifth billboard, but then disappearing right before the sixth and seventh.

**The marketing doesn't stop until the sales process has started.** *(And even then, it still doesn't stop.)*

This is why it's so important to be crystal clear on the journey you take people on and plan for any diversions, distractions and blockers on the way.

### PRO TIP: MARKETING ASSETS

Each touchpoint (whether there are seven, 25 or 100) should deliver something valuable to your chosen audience.

Once you achieve results for a good number of clients, you can take case studies, testimonials, results or client screenshots and turn them into marketing assets. Those assets will in turn feed the journey for others.

### MISTAKES TO AVOID

- ✗ Relying solely on social posts.
- ✗ Starting from the start, not the end.
- ✗ Not capitalising when people are hottest.

### ACTIONS TO TAKE NEXT

- ✓ Choose the right channel(s).
- ✓ Make sure all your touchpoints are clear.
- ✓ Fill in any potential gaps in the customer journey.

*If you think
you might be
overthinking it -
you are.*

# Chapter 5
# Content

Fear held me back for over 30 years.

Even though I understood there was real power in this 'personal brand' stuff, I did everything I could to avoid putting my face and name on my content.

I spent hours creating images and carousels. I made them on Canva first, then Photoshop, then PowerPoint (believe it or not), and then Adobe XD. You can imagine the length of time I spent on every slide being designed and perfected.

But I *refused* to put my face out there. I was scared of what people might say.

One night, I was putting my daughter to bed and decided to work on a carousel for a bit as she fell asleep. It was one about Wimbledon, and I reckon it's one of the best carousels I've ever made in terms of design and message.

After a while, I looked up from my work and realised I was still lying on her bedroom floor – *three hours later.*

What's worse is that, when I posted it, no one cared.

**I'd put in three hours of work for zero return.**

All these 'experts' were producing 10 times the amount of content I was. Horrendously designed and worded, some of the worst fucking content ever, but it didn't matter.

They were getting tens of thousands of followers (and probably hundreds of clients) because they were focused on *quantity* over quality.

It didn't matter that I had the most polished content, that it was absolutely beautiful and with the right message.

By focusing on quality over quantity, especially at the beginning, meant I ended up with fewer results and fewer clients.

My fear of judgement – and my perfectionism – were stopping me from achieving success. I lost out on months of potential connections, conversations, clients and cash because of that.

### *If you think you might be overthinking it – you are.*

The reality is that there's only so much planning you can do. People are going to say horrible things about your content or the fact you're trying to build a personal brand. They might even say it to your face. And there's nothing you can do about it.

Mainly, it's coming from a place of ignorance, fear or envy. Simply put, most people don't get it. Either they're scared to do it themselves or they think what you're doing is a mistake, and so they're trying to 'help' you.

A client recently told me, 'One of my husband's friends just called me a "LinkedIn wanker".'

And all I said was 'That's because you are. We all are.'

**Success breeds criticism.**

And that's okay.

We aren't here to seek validation; we're here to run a business.

A nice little sales reframe I use is this: 'Don't try to get a yes; try to get ten nos.' Give it a go. Put your face out there and try to get some criticism. See it as something to aim for.

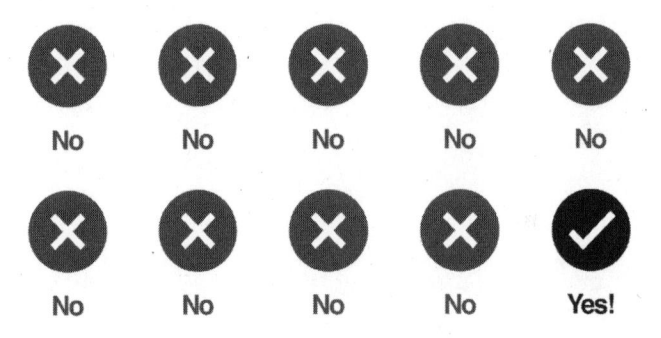

| ❌ | ❌ | ❌ | ❌ | ❌ |
|---|---|---|---|---|
| No | No | No | No | No |
| ❌ | ❌ | ❌ | ❌ | ✅ |
| No | No | No | No | Yes! |

***If you've not got any critics, you're not well-known enough.***

One of the best things that has come out of this journey – besides the connections, the money and the autonomy – is the fact that I'm completely true to who I am.

I'm not arsed about being validated by other people any more. (I am a bit, obviously; I post content to try to get people to like me.) But I can wholeheartedly take the piss out of myself, own my mistakes and talk publicly about any area of my life without feeling any kind of shame for it.

Whereas, a few years ago, I'd never have done that.

Once you can truly own who you are, the mistakes you've made and your flaws, you'll truly be at peace.

**And you can use it to drive yourself forwards.**

What you perceive as your flaws – the weird thing you do with your eyebrow, the fact you're a geek at heart, your stamp collection, etc. – will all appeal to other people because they're your point of differentiation.

**It's what will make you stand out.**

The attitude to take when doing anything like this is this: just go and do it. Do that *massive fucking thing*, and do it well. Only then will people start to respect you and pay attention.

Up until then, we're all going to be social media wankers.

So we might as well make some money whilst we do it.

## The purpose of content

The end goal of content is to generate leads.

Yes, there are secondary objectives, such as building awareness, getting downloads or sending people to our website. The best marketing does all of these things. But the *ultimate* aim of marketing is to get leads.

However, people aren't going to fucking jump out at you the minute you post. I'll keep repeating this until I'm blue in the face.

Organic marketing is a long-term play. So to get those leads, you have to take people on that journey we talked about in the last chapter. We've got to capture attention, build trust and ultimately, convert them.

And I'm going to show you how.

## Don't post and pray

People create a lot of crap content.

It's mainly because they create it without any intention or proper planning.

And that causes confusion for their audience. Instead, you need to consider these: What do you want people to do when they see your content? Why are you posting?

Which of these do you want them to do:

- → Buy?
- → Click?
- → Scroll?
- → Share?
- → Follow?
- → Download?
- → Feel something?
- → Watch for longer?
- → Change their view?
- → Believe something?

**Confused people don't buy.**

If you don't know what you want your content to do, your audience won't either.

So set your intention for every piece of content.

## Begin at the end

When you understand what you want your content to do, you eliminate the guesswork (for you *and* your audience).

That's why I recommend being *intentional* with *every* piece of content. Plan every step, rather than leaving it to chance.

**In other words, begin with the end in mind and reverse-engineer your content.**

(We spoke about this concept in the previous chapter. If you missed that, go back and read it again.)

Here's the exact process I use, which makes content creation super easy:

1. → **Choose an objective for the post**
2. → **Align the objective with a call to action (CTA)**
3. → **Decide on a topic / pillar**
4. → **Write a strong hook / headline**
5. → **Choose a format & create the content**

## Step 1. Objectives

Every piece of content should meet one of the three objectives in the CTC method:

- Capture
- Trust
- Convert

## 'Capture' content

Capturing attention means creating posts with a broad appeal. It's content that 'captures' as many people as possible so you can turn that attention into new followers. You want as many people as possible to know who you are and what you do.

### Capture examples

**Time: A Universal Concept**

**Well-Known Brands & Images**

## 'Trust' content

Buyers have to trust you before they'll buy from you, and it's this part of the 'journey' that a lot of your followers and audience will undertake.

Members of your target audience will be looking for reasons to trust you before they buy, which you can do by posting about your business and your personal life. (As much as you're happy to share, obviously).

## *Trust examples*

Personal: Taking Time Off

Detailed Process & Outcome

## 'Convert' content

Convert content sits at the very bottom of the journey (or the triangle in the last chapter). Typically, it only applies to a certain percentage of your audience: the ones who are almost ready to buy or are sitting on the fence.

Posts that aim to convert should focus on logical messaging: 'Buy my thing' or 'Book a call'. And because of that, conversion content will get much lower engagement – but that doesn't mean it isn't working.

## Convert examples

↓
Client Interview with call CTA

↓
Price Rise Promo

Your content won't always fit neatly into one of those three categories; there will be plenty of times when the categories for the content overlap. But whatever category you choose, it'll depend on what phase you're in.

My main objective is, of course, to generate leads, and it'll probably be the same for most people reading this book.

But you don't get leads trying to convert people *all the time.*

As we've already discussed, everything is a journey. You can't just put one post out and expect people to buy; you'll need to post a mix of capture, trust and convert content.

It's like Gary Vee's advice, which basically says you jab, jab, jab, then you smack 'em with the right hook.[9]

**Jab** → Capture attention

**Jab** → Build trust

**Jab** → Build more trust

**Right hook** → Convert

**Jab** → Add value

**Jab** → Share something personal

**Jab** → Add more value

**Right hook** → Convert

Leave space in your calendar for **reactive content** too.

This means giving yourself the freedom to play and test something new. There are loads of trends in marketing, and there will be some you'll want to hop on board with and adapt to your own style. There might be one day a week when you've got nothing planned, and so you want to post something without too much thought. It might just be the fact that you have to wait until the day of posting to grab the image or video you need.

Reactive content is your buffer, and it should make up about 10% of your content.

> ## PRO TIP: TRENDS
>
> I tend to avoid them.
>
> They come and go, but the fundamentals always stay the same. You could put hours into mastering a trend only for it to not be relevant next week.
>
> So don't fall into the trap of changing your whole strategy just to look relevant in the short term.

*A little content hack*

You don't ever have to start with a blank page, even though you'll feel like that at the start.

But if you do get stuck, here's a tip:

**Document, don't create.**

Talk about what you've just done. Open up your calendar and literally base a post on something that happened that week.

It doesn't have to be all the tips, tricks and formulas. The best content is sometimes the least polished and the most authentic, and it automatically meets the trust-building objective.

## Step 2. Choose your call to action (CTA)

Once you know your objective, it's time to choose your CTA.

There's no point grabbing your prospect's attention with a well-written post or a pretty picture if you've got nowhere to take them.

**Tell them what to do and get them *to take action.***

Obviously, you're not going to put the CTA at the start of your content, but *before* you create the content, you should know what it'll be. It eliminates the guesswork and means you can work backwards to create the topic.

Including a CTA might seem obvious, but it's an important part of content creation that *so many people get wrong.*

When Amy and I sit down to watch Netflix, we sometimes take half an hour to make a decision on which film to choose: it's analysis paralysis. There are so many options out there that, by the time we've chosen one, one of us will fall asleep within five minutes of actually watching.

The thing is that if we only had two dusty old DVDs, the choice would be much simpler.

The point of having a clear and simple CTA is to give people *direction and reduce distraction.*

If the objective is to drive newsletter downloads or call bookings, tell your audience that's what you want them to do. If you don't, they'll call themselves to action and move on.

One major mistake that people make is that they try to do everything with one piece of content.

Yes, you may have multiple objectives, but you can't push people in 17 different directions and expect a result.

Asking them to 'Like this post. And share it. And book a call. And buy my course. And download my free e-book. And do this. And do that.' Is it any wonder that most of these posts don't get results?

Giving people one to two clear routes is much more powerful than asking them to do everything or being too vague.

Here are some examples of bad CTAs:

- ✗ 'DM me for more info.'
- ✗ 'What do you think?'
- ✗ 'Let's talk.'
- ✗ No CTA.

These don't work because they're too vague, they don't make it easy for people to respond or they're just bad practice.

What about some examples of good CTAs?

- ✓ 'Follow me to learn how to [what you teach].'
- ✓ 'Coaches, want three productivity tips delivered to your email inbox every Monday? Join 500 others and sign up to my newsletter below.'
- ✓ 'Would you like 10x your revenue without [pain point]? Drop me a DM including the word "CLIENTS" now.'

You can see that these are very specific and very outcome focused.

### PRO TIP: START NOW

Draft your own set of CTAs for capture, trust and convert content. Then you can copy and paste them into your posts to save time.

Check out some of my CTAs on my LinkedIn or Instagram posts for ideas to get you started.

Don't assume people know what they need to do, how to do it or where they need to go next. You're engineering *every* part of the journey down to the smallest detail, so please, for the love of God, give them a clear CTA.

> ### PRO TIP: TIME
>
> The problem a lot of people face with this part of the process is that it requires thinking upfront, which most of us just don't want to do.
>
> What I'm showing you is going to save you time, but people don't look at this like that. They only go with the short-term view of 'I'll just post whatever's in my head now,' which is why most people's content ends up being shite.
>
> This is why we're going through this in a sequential, methodical order.
>
> If you create a system that takes you 10 hours up front, but it reduces content production time by 60%, you'll save much more time and get better results in the mid-to-long term.
>
> So take the time to understand this information and use it, and I promise you'll be able to create the outcome you want.

## Step 3. Content pillars/topics

People shit themselves when they hear the phrase **'content pillars'**, but they're just a set of guidelines for things to post about.

Nothing more than that.

And they can be changed at any time.

It's not a hard and fast rule, but your pillars are there to help you stay on topic, and they should give you that freedom to talk about stuff that's relevant to you and your business.

There are three content pillars I recommend using:

- Me and mine
- Mindset
- Mastery

**Me and mine:** Personal stuff such as your journey, family, past, hobbies, successes, failures, likes and interests.

**Mindset**: Topics specific to your psychology and the mindset of your target audience – such as your worries, fears, hopes, questions, habits and objections.

**Mastery**: Your expertise. What you're selling. The outcomes you offer. Your processes. Your clients' results.

Under each of these pillars will be certain topics that you can talk about repeatedly.

Here are mine:

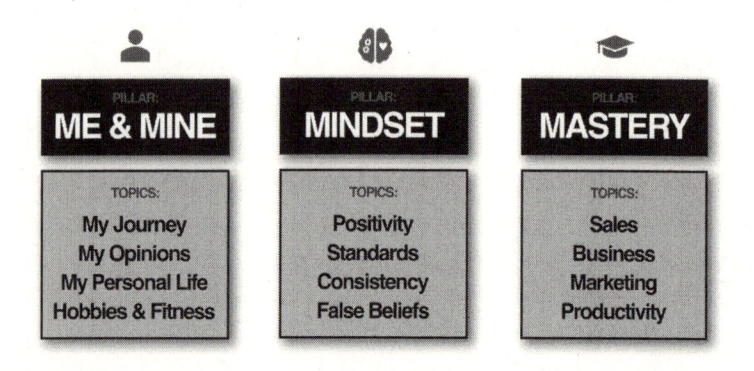

| PILLAR: ME & MINE | PILLAR: MINDSET | PILLAR: MASTERY |
|---|---|---|
| TOPICS: | TOPICS: | TOPICS: |
| My Journey | Positivity | Sales |
| My Opinions | Standards | Business |
| My Personal Life | Consistency | Marketing |
| Hobbies & Fitness | False Beliefs | Productivity |

Everyone's pillars and topics will be different, and you can break every single one down into an unlimited number of ideas.

Take a moment now to create your own content pillars.

Don't spend hours on this; it'll never be perfect. It's just to get you started. You don't need to go into too much detail either. In fact, the wider, the better.

## PRO TIP: INTENTIONAL CONTENT

Your content should make people either:

- Feel something (emotion)
- Believe something (logic)
- Both

**LOGICAL** *Think*   **EMOTIONAL** *Feel*

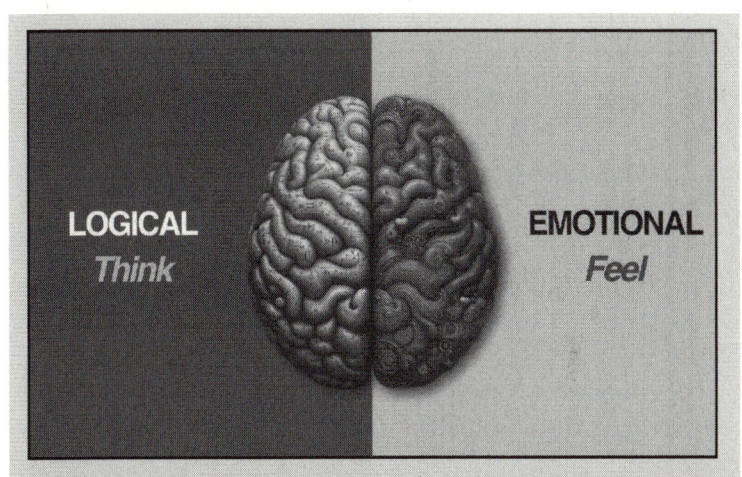

This is what will drive action and purchasing decisions. Be sure to cover a mix of emotional and logical topics in your posts.

Logical topics include these:

- Information
- Processes
- Product
- Proof

Emotional content could be:

- Storytelling
- Personal life
- Behind the scenes

## Step 4. Write the hook

**Don't underestimate the importance of a good hook.**

It's the first line or two of your content. It's your headline, and its job is to *attract and retain attention*.

If you don't capture someone's attention in the first few seconds, they're gone.

A lot of people say the hook should be 80% of your effort, because without attention, you have nothing. The rest of the content is pointless.

It's like a newspaper headline, which is designed to create intrigue or excitement. In some cases, it's to scare you. In other cases, it's something polarising or controversial.

I'm not saying write something horrible just for attention – that's not authentic or good marketing. But think about ways of pulling on people's emotions and curiosity to get them to stop and look at your post.

As a guide, the best headlines are the following:

- ✓ Short, specific and unique.
- ✓ They create a feeling of fear of missing out (FOMO), curiosity or intrigue.
- ✓ They use numbers, time or something very specific/tangible.
- ✓ They always deliver on the promise. (Otherwise, you're just writing clickbait.)

Here are some examples:

| Bad Headline | Good Headline |
|---|---|
| Time management tips → | How I save 7 hours a week (and you can too) |
| My client's killing it → | My client made £6,000 in 4 hours by doing this: |
| Wanna work with me? → | I'm gonna work with 2 people free this month… |

Can you see how a good hook gets your attention and a bad one doesn't?

I'm a big fan of bold or negative headlines that tend to focus on pain points or suggest ways of moving away from them:

- ✓ 'This one thing is costing you thousands.'
- ✓ 'The reason I stopped doing ABC is…'
- ✓ 'For the love of God, don't do XYZ.'

I also like to talk about universal topics such as time and money. They're broad enough to be relevant to everyone, but they're also specific enough that my target audience can relate to them. And they're both areas my service helps to improve.

**Find your preferred style and make it part of your personal brand.**

Avoid hooks that are too airy-fairy, too business focused or just so broad that they don't feel relevant to anyone.

Think about what's important to your target audience:

- → What would your clients be curious about?
- → What are their pain points and desires?
- → What questions do they ask?
- → What's intriguing to them?

Writing hooks is a skill, and it'll take time, so don't expect to be perfect at these when you start.

## PRO TIP: TEST

Everything in marketing is about testing.

You can't predict how an audience will respond, but if you're selling to a specific group of people, they probably all have similar likes and dislikes.

So if certain headlines aren't attracting the right attention, see that as feedback that you need to work on your hooks.

## Step 5. Find the format and create

Different platforms tend to reward different formats. The different formats you can use (at the time of writing this book) are these:

- Carousels
- Live videos
- Text-only posts
- Short-form video (under 60 seconds)
- Single image posts (photos and graphics)
- Long-form video (60 seconds – 60 minutes)

Looking at this list objectively, we can break it down into three formats:

**Words** · **Images** · **Videos**

And yes, for the nitpickers, audio is a format too, but we're not covering it in this book. Soz.

*Writing, design and video*

**1. Writing**

Use the ABC framework to help you structure your content:

**A** → **Attention**

**B** → **Breakdown**

**C** → **Call to Action**

**A → Attention:** Capture it using a good hook.

**B → Breakdown:** Break down the topic you're discussing.

**C → Call to action:** Your chosen CTA.

Make sure there's lots of white space in your post. No one wants to read a block of text, because they'll get bored. And break up that writing with bullet points, emojis, short sentences, long sentences, one line at a time, two lines at a time or three lines at a time.

**2. Design**

Pick your neutral base colours and highlight colours, and then stick to them. Basically, these are your brand colours.

Don't go too colourful as it can make your design overwhelming and hard to read.

With design, make sure to include lots of white space and ensure your text and other elements aren't hitting the sides of the images.

Don't use a million different fonts either. Stick to one body font that's easy to read and one headline font that's bold and attention-grabbing. Make sure they balance and complement each other. Don't choose fonts that look mismatched.

If you're using a photo, you want it to be well lit. And don't overuse filters.

In fact, don't overthink design. If you're a newbie, just use Canva. There are hundreds of templates on there.

### 3. Video

If you want to do video, you don't need a big, fancy set-up – you're not a YouTuber just yet, my friend. Stand in front of a window, facing it so you've got the light on your face, and use your phone to record it.

Make sure your audio is as good as the video. If you're aiming to edit your video, I'd recommend cutting out every single gasp, stutter or stammer.

I've found it's better to have a script or bullet points and read each part line by line until it's delivered correctly.

## Always keep testing

Marketing is one big testing game, so make sure you're aware of the format that works best on your chosen channel. From month to month, things will change. You may find out that Instagram prefers to push carousels versus video. And then, a couple of months later, you'll find that carousels don't get as much reach or interactions, but video does.

Each format has its own pros and cons, and you'll be better at some and worse at others – whether you know it or not.

The real lesson here is this: don't try to learn a bunch of new stuff straight away. Instead, *play to your strengths*. If you're crap on camera, don't do video to start. If you're better at writing, stick with text posts. If you can't design, then just use photos. Just literally go through your camera roll and find a picture, even if it's from three years ago.

**If you're new to making content, take the path of least resistance.**

That probably means avoiding filming videos or designing graphics – stick with photos and text. Obviously, this will be platform dependent, but photos and text are generally the easiest to do.

You can always build your design and video skills up in the background.

## Cadence

A question I get asked a hell of a lot from people who haven't done this before is this: how frequently should I publish content?

I publish every day.

Some people publish twice a day.

Other people do it a couple of times a week.

**The real answer can only be dictated by you: post as often as is sustainable for you.**

| Type | Mon | Tue | Wed | Thu | Fri | Sat | Sun |
|---|---|---|---|---|---|---|---|
| Minimum | ✓ |  | ✓ |  | ✓ |  |  |
| Working Week | ✓ | ✓ | ✓ | ✓ | ✓ |  |  |
| Recommended | ✓ | ✓ | ✓ | ✓ | ✓ | ✓ | ✓ |
| Ultimate | ✓✓ | ✓✓ | ✓✓ | ✓✓ | ✓✓ | ✓✓ | ✓✓ |

If you're not going to be able to maintain seven posts a week for the next two years, don't ever bother starting there. You're just setting yourself up for failure.

For beginners, I'd recommend about three to five times a week. But if you've been doing it for a while and you're confident, you can churn more out and step it up to five to seven.

But only commit to what you can maintain.

To make things easier, I suggest our clients tie each day to a theme – either an objective, a format or a topic.

**Example A** → Objectives: Convert content on Tuesdays & Thursdays.

**Example B** → Formats: Video posts on Mondays & Fridays.

**Example C** → Topic: Personal content on Tuesdays & Saturdays.

You don't have to do this, but I found it reduces the number of decisions, each of which drains the personal battery we mentioned.

---

### PRO TIP: PLATFORMS

Publishing frequency will be platform dependent.

Some platforms will suffocate your reach if you post more than once a day, whereas others will reward multiple daily posts.

Do your research.

## Timing

Aim to publish your content around the time most of your audience are likely to be active on the platform. Again, different platforms will respond in different ways, so this will require some testing.

If you've got international clients, what time are they most likely to be online? Do most of your ideal clients have children? If so, then you probably want to avoid the time of the school run.

What about weekends? I post on weekends, but a lot of people don't. The reason I do is because I want to be as consistent as hell and there's also less competition for eyeballs on a Sunday. Again, do what's sustainable for you.

If you get stuck, look at what other people in your space are doing.

### MISTAKES TO AVOID

- ✗ Overthinking it.
- ✗ Focusing on quality rather than quantity – for now.
- ✗ Publishing on every single channel; instead, master one at a time.

### ACTIONS TO TAKE NEXT

- ✓ Plan your content pillars.
- ✓ Choose the easiest format to post.
- ✓ Reverse-engineer and write your post.

- ✓ Schedule it to publish at a time your prospects will be online.
- ✓ Do it *now*!

---

### PRO TIP: IMPROVE YOUR COPY SKILLS

Copywriting (writing to promote, sell or get attention) is the most overlooked and undervalued skill. Even when you're on video, the words you use need to be intentional.

You can have all the fancy diagrams you want, the nicest layout, great carousels and all the motion graphics on the videos, but this all comes down to writing more than anything else.

It's a skill necessary for great marketing, and if it's something you're not confident with or good at yet, that's okay.

Be ready to sit down and practice it, just like any other skill.

Look at top copywriters and study their posts.

## Bonus: Scheduling, publishing and engagement

It's usually best to publish content at a time when you're going to be online to engage with any comments and, in a way, warm up the algorithm.

Don't just post and ghost – you should be ready to engage.

Social media has the word 'social' in it for a reason. There's nothing worse than being that person who only shows up when they want something. If you're only showing up to post, and you're not giving anything back by engaging with anyone else, your posts are probably going to fall flat.

Organic marketing is getting harder by the day.

If you want to direct attention to your profile and posts, adopt an outbound approach and comment on other people's posts too.

### PRO TIP: TARGETED LISTS

| Influencers | Peers | Ideal Clients | Supporters |

> Have a list of people that you actively want to engage with. That list should consist of a few types of people:
>
> **Influencers:** These are people in your space who already have the audience you want.
>
> **Peers**: People who are on a similar level to you. Some of them may even fall into the category of 'competitors'. Engaging with them will ultimately help you because you want their audience too!
>
> **Ideal clients:** Don't just DM them. Have conversations with them outside the inbox too by commenting on their posts. It's a great way to start a relationship.
>
> **Supporters:** These are people that you can't necessarily sell to but who come and support you all the time. Spend some time giving back!

If you know you need to publish your post at 8am every day, you should aim to be online at 8am, if possible.

If you can't, then that's when you can use scheduling tools.

I'm a big advocate for scheduling and having content ready well in advance.

It's incredibly helpful to schedule content ahead of time, especially if your target clients live in a different country, when you go on holiday or simply if you're on the school run when the post needs to come out.

For most social channels, you can schedule natively using the platform itself. Alternatively, you can use a scheduling tool. Buffer, Hootsuite and Later are just some you can use at the time of writing this.

Even though my content is posted across multiple channels, we still batch and schedule all of it natively rather than using a tool because a lot of these social platforms tend not to favour third-party software.

I've heard mixed reports of using tools, so do what works for you.

If you need to use a scheduling tool because you have international clients or you want to save time, then do it. Just be aware that it might affect things a bit.

## Engagement

When you leave a comment on someone else's post, don't just put a fire emoji or say, 'Great share,' and think that's enough.

Leave informative and insightful comments.

If your comment is interesting enough, people are going to check out your profile and start looking at your content too. Hopefully, some of those people will turn into followers and, eventually, leads.

It's always best to be constructive with whatever you say. Whether you agree or disagree, say why. Has something similar happened to you? Can you talk about it from your point of view? Do you want to offer some form of compliment? Is there an extra point you can add in that the creator may have missed?

Don't just engage for the sake of it.

Find something in the post you can comment on authentically or use to carry on the conversation. It might sound a bit painful, but trust me, it's a necessary evil. And it's blatant when people engage without actually caring at all.

The more your following grows, the more you'll start to see this on your own posts as well.

Engagement also means responding to people who take time out of their day to comment on your post. You may go out there and get all the attention you want, but if you post content and you get questions, compliments and comments underneath your posts, and then you don't respond, you'll look arrogant.

True engagement can lead to real conversations.

And that's the start of people knowing, liking and trusting you – which, ultimately, means leads for your pipeline.

We'll cover what to do with these leads in the next chapter.

# Chapter 6
# Leads

The *biggest* problem business owners in this space have is also the thing they avoid the most:

**Lead generation.**

There are so many struggling and failed small businesses out there, and it's because they avoid the real work.

To keep things simple, anyone who's a potential customer is a 'lead'.

And *every* business needs to generate leads to survive.

Take McDonald's.

Everyone knows what the company is.

But it *still* works on generating leads.

It spends hundreds of millions of pounds on advertising every year to promote new products and new locations. It works constantly on raising awareness with the aim of increasing footfall to its restaurants; taking people on that journey we discussed.

Why?

**Because successful companies understand the power of staying front of mind.**

Without leads, you don't have sales opportunities…

Without sales opportunities, you don't have clients…

Without clients, you don't have a business…

Without a business, you don't have money…

Without money…

You can go as far as you want with this sequence.

If the big brands are putting in the work, *so should you*. There will be hard times ahead if you don't.

## Building a lead-generation mindset

We work with a lot of corporate escapees. Typically, when they leave full-time employment, they'll land a few clients quite easily – usually from their existing network of peers and ex-colleagues.

**But they rarely ever market or push themselves to generate more leads.**

They focus on what they *think* are bigger priorities, such as delivering and fulfilling their services.

And they're not completely wrong, but…

When they've exhausted that network of people they can sell to immediately, they're back down to zero. They've not been doing anything to fill up their pipeline of opportunities.

**Successful business owners *always* have an eye on lead-generating activities.**

There's a rule I learned years ago in the world of sales and marketing: anyone you approach or interact with today probably won't become a client or even maybe a lead for 30–90 days.

But people give up because they don't see instant results.

Just like planting seeds to harvest later, these conversations and these relationships take time to grow. Some of them, if they're watered correctly and get enough sunlight, will come to fruition. And some won't.

### *You don't eat the fruit the day you plant the seed.*

Lead generation is a volume and consistency thing more than anything else.

It's essential to be consistent in planting those seeds, and planting *a lot of them*. Plant them on rainy days and on sunny days. On days you feel great and days you feel shit.

Consistently generating leads for your business requires a certain mindset.

Being clear on *why* you are doing this will help you to endure the shit days. Because you *will* experience peaks, troughs, ups, downs, rough and smooth on this journey.

Your success is all up to you, so get clear on where you want to go, who you want to be and how you're going to get there.

I'm not a woo-woo kinda guy. I don't like to talk about vision boards. But this is an opportunity to act like your future self.

Is your future self a business owner who makes lots of money and lots of profit? Is your future self someone who isn't afraid of going and speaking to people and generating leads?

That's the type of person you need to become. But not in the future. *Today.* Because deep down, you already have what it takes to be that person…

Someone who doesn't quit.

## PRO TIP: DUNNING–KRUGER EFFECT

What most people do when they build a new business is go on the journey in this image:

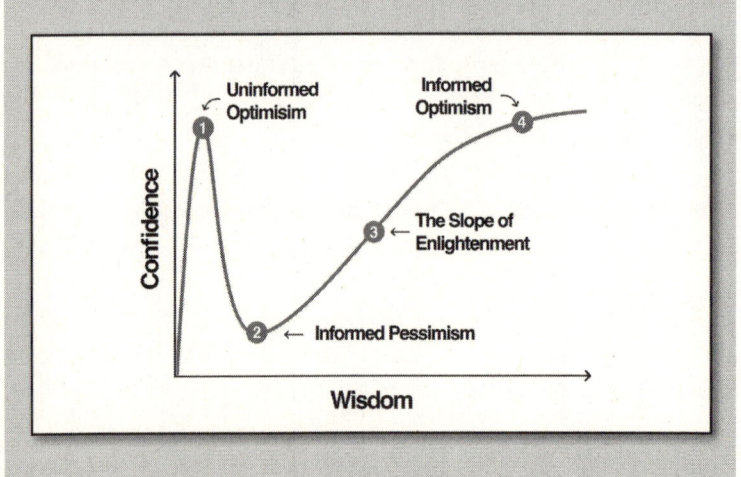

**Phase 1:** When people are in the early stages, they're excited to build their new business. They're enthusiastic and full of energy, but they're ignorant of what they don't know: **'uninformed optimism'.**

**Phase 2:** People soon realise how difficult running a business actually is, and they very quickly descend into the **'valley of despair'**. *This is where most people quit.* They're now fully aware of the hard work required and enter what's known as **'informed pessimism'**.

**Please expect this and be aware when you hit this phase, and then remind yourself not to quit.**

**Phase 3:** Those who don't quit begin to climb **'the slope of enlightenment'**. And slowly but surely, their confidence grows alongside their level of skill.

**Phase 4:** This phase is known as **'the plateau of sustainability'**. They enter informed optimism. They're aware of the challenges ahead and can run their business sustainably. They've reached a level of expertise. They know how to win, but they've also acquired the knowledge of how not to lose.

If you're new to generating leads, expect to go through this part of the journey (maybe a few times too). It's a *normal* part of business.

It's something we see frequently inside C2C. The highest performers have all ridden this wave.

## How to generate leads

**Lead generation** means creating interest for your service with the goal of turning that interest into a sale.

And those leads can come to you in two ways: **outbound** and **inbound**.

### Inbound

Inbound leads are when people reach out to you first and indicate they want to take the conversation/sales opportunity further. They could DM you, leave a comment on a post or go straight to booking a call through your website.

You may have found some success with inbound queries from your existing network or referrals, but this isn't likely to be the case forever.

You're (probably) going to have to go outbound as well.

### Outbound

Outbound is when *you* start the conversation. It can either be **one-to-one** or **one-to-many**.

There are loads of ways to go outbound when generating leads, and content is one of the easiest ways to do it.

But the problem with relying on content to bring you leads is that only 5%–10% of your audience will be in that buying window and ready to convert.

Everyone else is either completely irrelevant or they're not ready – *yet*.

So you have to do the work to increase the percentage of people sitting in that buying window, alongside moving the existing people closer to a sales exchange.

Here are 14 different examples of how you can generate leads:

1. DMs
2. Radio
3. Affiliates
4. Paid ads
5. Podcasts
6. Websites
7. SMS lists
8. Cold calls
9. Press features
10. Masterclasses
11. Lead magnets
12. Emails (cold/warm)
13. Social media content
14. Referrals/introductions

For the purpose of this book, we're going to talk in-depth about DMs and a concept I've coined called 'one-time assets' (OTAs). This is because they're *the easiest for you to control*.

We can't control the press or radio, and we can't control social media platforms. We may post content on social media, but we aren't in charge of the platform itself. Referrals aren't guaranteed, and we probably can't rely on splashing out thousands on paid advertising at the start either.

**What we *can* control are DMs and OTAs.**

If you've worked through *Chapter 3. Traction*, you'll have seen the power of having conversations. That's how you can start generating those leads easily: having conversations with as many people as possible, as consistently as possible.

## One-time assets (OTAs)

An OTA is something you buy, build or create once that lives forever.

These are things such as brand guidelines, standard operating procedures, dashboards and systems.

**For this chapter, I'm going to focus on OTAs from a lead-generation perspective, as I believe they have the highest return on time.**

They're a one-to-many method of communication. Some examples specifically for lead generation are these:

- DM scripts
- Lead magnets
- Evergreen content
- Client results / case studies
- Welcome/follow-up sequences

These assets will be things you build once, but they can be served to an unlimited number of people to generate interest and, hopefully, lead to inbound enquiries or help with outbound conversations.

Let's look at some examples.

## Example 1. Evergreen content

**Evergreen content** is probably the best example of an OTA to generate leads, and you can use what you learned in *Chapter 5* to create yours.

When you craft evergreen content, it's worth spending more time on it than a normal piece of content because it'll likely be used over and over again. It's something you should be able to post once every few months that'll always be relevant and bring in leads.

Recently, I wrote and filmed a video breaking down how one of my clients made €250k using LinkedIn. That video is an OTA I can do this with:

- → Post on YouTube, where it'll be searchable for several years into the future and where anyone can find it.
- → Feature on my website for social proof.
- → Send automatically in email sequences.
- → Post once every four to six months across short-form platforms such as LinkedIn and Instagram.
- → Use as part of our sales process once prospects have booked calls with us.

It's a piece of evergreen content that I can keep in rotation and use to start/continue conversations at any time – forever.

## Example 2. Lead magnets

A **lead magnet** is the perfect example of an OTA.

You provide a pre-recorded video lesson, cheat sheet, course or tool for free in exchange for someone's email address.

Once you have their email address, you can market to them. Either through regular marketing emails such as a newsletter, specific sales emails or a sequence that sends automatically when they download an OTA.

And that's the beauty of OTAs: you build them once, but they can work for you time and time again – even if you're asleep!

## Example 3. DM bank

I like to keep a list of DMs that get positive responses, plus well-phrased questions to ask that get good responses.

I keep them easily accessible so I can copy and paste them regularly when having DM conversations. This way, when you're speaking to people, you can save hours (and don't get stuck on what to say). This **DM bank** can be handed to a VA too, which means they'll write in the same way as you when messaging prospects.

## OTA principles

- → Don't make them time bound or topical. If you're making evergreen content, it should be relevant 24/7/365.
- → Make OTAs for tasks or processes you find yourself repeating. If you perform the same task regularly – such as sending follow-up emails or constantly educating people on what you do – create OTAs you can put in rotation regularly to save you time.

Don't be afraid to make a sacrifice in the short term in order to satisfy the long term. Putting the effort in to make OTAs will serve you time and time again, but repeating the grunt work won't.

## Having conversations that convert

***Opportunity is everywhere, but it sits on the other side of a conversation.***

Conversations can start anywhere at any time. You might get a cold inbound enquiry, or someone might see one of your OTAs and get in touch. But in the beginning, more often than not, you'll be the one starting the conversation. (There's a list of *when* you'd start the conversation later in this chapter.)

We're going to focus specifically on DMs.

Human conversation is a massive topic, so I'm just going to show you the stages of a good DM exchange and a few examples, rather than go into too much detail.

There are *three* main stages to go through when you start a conversation using DMs:

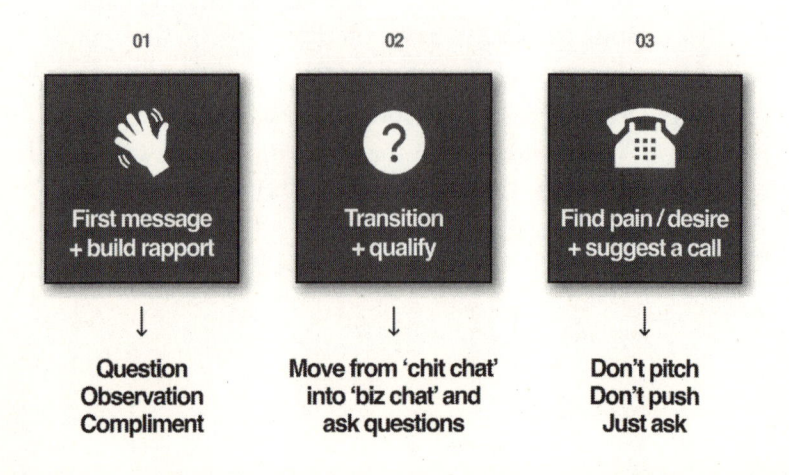

| 01 | 02 | 03 |
|---|---|---|
| 👋 | ❓ | ☎️ |
| First message + build rapport | Transition + qualify | Find pain / desire + suggest a call |
| ↓ | ↓ | ↓ |
| Question<br>Observation<br>Compliment | Move from 'chit chat' into 'biz chat' and ask questions | Don't pitch<br>Don't push<br>Just ask |

## Stage 1. First message and build rapport

I've always found it best to start DMs with a question, a compliment or an observation (or all three).

*Examples*

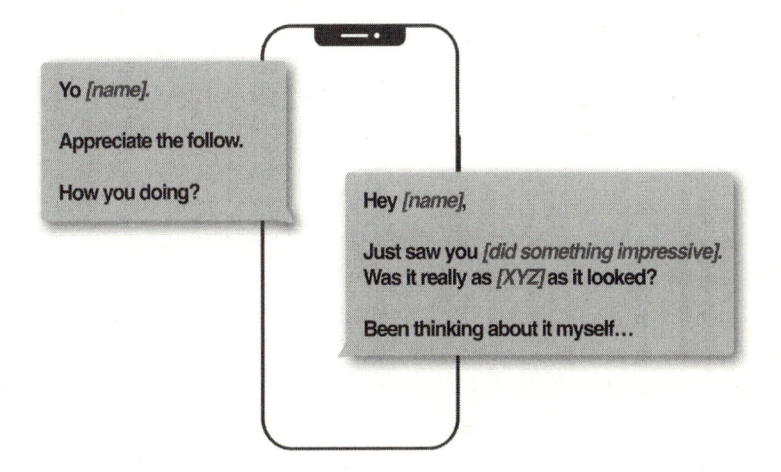

> Yo *[name]*,
>
> Appreciate the follow.
>
> How you doing?

> Hey *[name]*,
>
> Just saw you *[did something impressive]*. Was it really as *[XYZ]* as it looked?
>
> Been thinking about it myself…

The aim of the first message isn't to sell, it's to get a reply. This reply will enable you to have a bit of back and forth to build rapport. If you don't get a reply, the conversation ends there, which is why questions work so well. Don't try to book a call or convert people straight away.

Building trust takes time.

So view this as exactly what it is: a conversation. Nothing more.

Every interaction you have with potential clients should make that person feel like they matter. So treat each conversation like it's your most important one, rather than just viewing people as numbers.

Trust me when I say this: being truly genuine shines through.

## Stage 2. Transition and qualify

Once you've lowered the prospect's guard, you can slowly transition to talking about business (or your area of expertise) and then find out more about their situation to suss out if they're a good fit for a call.

*Transition examples*

> How long have you been [XYZ]?

> Have we spoken before? No? In that case, what do you do?

> I saw you mention [XYZ] — how did that happen?

## Stage 3. Uncover their pain point / desire and suggest a call

Once you've found a reason why/how you could help them, simply ask if they're open to a call. You don't have to be pushy about it either.

*Example*

> I hate to be forward, but would love to hop on a call with you. I've helped lots of *[audience]* achieve *[goal]*.

> Good question. More than happy to help you out further with this. Have you got time for a call *[this week]*?

> If you're open to it, I'd love to jump on a call, offer some advice on *[problem]* and show you how I've taken my clients from *[X to Y]*. Do you have some time *[on Tuesday]*?

Use these as inspiration, but remember to make these questions your own.

If the prospect agrees to a call, send them to your calendar software to schedule it.

## Five key points to remember

### Point 1.

Generating leads is *not* about selling. It's about these:

- Qualifying potential clients
- Opening up opportunities
- Nurturing relationships
- Warming up prospects
- Exploring options

**This is about doing the work *before* the sale.**

We aren't entering into every conversation by trying to sell from the get-go. You're just having a chat and nothing more. If that chat then opens up a sales opportunity, then sure, jump on it.

But try to enter these exchanges with no agenda and no expectations.

The worst thing you can do is pitch a call to someone before you've found out more about their situation. Try to lower the prospect's guard and show them that you're *normal*.

## Point 2.

The journey from the first message to booking a call won't be linear.

Be ready for your conversations to skip around. You might go backwards or skip a stage. It could take three days, 10 days or even a year. It once took me 12 months to convert a client. Be patient. This is a long game.

## Point 3.

It's all well and good starting conversations and just having a chat, but if you don't progress to the 'biz chat' stage quickly, you end up in 'the friend zone'. This is the last thing you want.

Be extremely intentional in your conversations.

Suggest more calls, and you'll get more calls booked. The more you do, the more calls are attended, the more you improve and the more clients you win.

## Point 4.

This is easier said than done, but try to *decrease* the emotional attachment you have to each conversation. If you only have one opportunity in the pipeline, that's a lot of pressure for you to convert. It'll occupy 100% of your headspace.

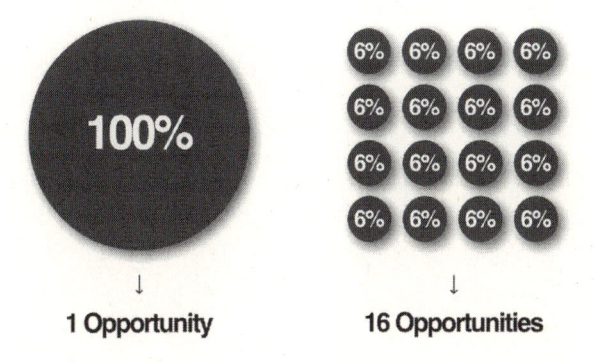

100%
↓
**1 Opportunity**

6% × 16
↓
**16 Opportunities**

But if you have 16 opportunities in the pipeline, your emotional attachment is spread across those 16 people, and it doesn't matter if one, five or even 10 of them don't convert. Good lead generation means you're constantly refilling that pipeline with leads.

**That's why you need to have conversations every day.**

### Point 5.

This whole section is just a framework.

Adapt it to your own style, and if you don't have a style yet, that's okay. You probably haven't done enough reps.

Put the reps in, and your style and confidence will follow. Remember the Dunning–Kruger effect.

## The 4C workflow

Now you know about OTAs and using DMs, let's dive deeper.

We're going to talk about something I call the '4C workflow'. We touched on it in *Chapter 4*.

This workflow, like most things, is based on consistency, but I want to show you exactly what I recommend that our clients do each day.

The workflow looks like this:

- → Content
- → Comments
- → Connections
- → Conversations

It'll need to be executed day in and day out, and it'll help you stay front of mind and connect with the relevant people.

> This is specific to LinkedIn, but you can adapt it to most social platforms

## Content

We covered the importance of content in *Chapter 5*. But as a reminder, posting regular content that inspires, informs or entertains will help you to capture attention and build trust you can then convert into leads.

## Comments

We already discussed why commenting is an important part of your content strategy, but it's also essential for lead generation. I can go and comment on one of Gary Vee's posts, not because I care too much about commenting, but because I want to hijack the audience attention that he already has.

People will see my comments (which will be authentic, relevant and useful), and that'll lead people to come and check out my profile, and then connect or follow me. This then allows me to start a conversation.

I suggest commenting on about 20 accounts a day, and it should be a mix of potential clients, peers and influencers in your space, which we touched on in the last chapter.

## Connections

You should top up your audience constantly.

Send 20 connection requests a day to your ideal clients, influencers in your space and people who have the audience that you want, which may include competitors, peers and other people in your industry.

## Conversations

This is where the bulk of your lead generation and nurturing will happen. Feel free to use the structure I've just shown to you.

Ideally, you should start conversations with anyone who's done one of these:

- Followed you
- Liked your post
- Viewed your profile
- Looks like a perfect fit
- Posted content you like
- Commented on your post
- Downloaded a lead magnet
- Accepted a connection request
- Requested to connect with you
- Followed one of your competitors
- Become part of the same community as you

Use any of these opportunities to start a conversation.

If you're feeling confident, you can go out and speak to people cold. But it all depends on the amount of attention you'll gain and how ruthless you want to be; a lot of people don't appreciate cold messages.

The good news is that you can outsource a lot of this workflow when the time is right, and you could also drop elements of it too. But I urge you to take this process and make it your own.

> ### PRO TIP: DO THE WORK
>
> Buying this book doesn't entitle you to leads.
>
> **I can give you the tools and the knowledge, but you have to put in the work.**
>
> You'll have off days. Some days will be slow; other days, you'll fly. Some days, it'll be hard; other days, it'll be easy. But I'm telling you now that this is what matters.
>
> *This* **is the work.**
>
> You don't shoot a gun twice and suddenly become an expert marksman. It's the consistency of shooting day in, day out; that's when you see results.
>
> That's why this workflow needs to become a daily part of your routine.

## Don't forget the data

There are two huge mistakes business owners make when it comes to lead generation:

1. They act based on their emotions.
2. They focus on the wrong thing.

## Emotion vs logic

Lots of people think lead generation and sales is an art. That it's about smooth talking or being a pushy car salesman: Matilda's-dad-style vibes.

Actually, it's much more of a science.

**It's data focused.**

Steven Bartlett (*Diary of a CEO*) and his team test over 100 thumbnails for every video release of his podcast – and that's in the first hour.

They do this because they want data.

When you have data, you can make decisions that are going to improve your business, rather than relying on guesswork.

If you don't have data in your business, chances are you're acting emotionally. Doing what *feels* right, rather than acting and doing what you *know* is right.

If you're not tracking data, you're running your business emotionally, and that's not a good way to get the results you want.

## Input vs output

Most people make the mistake of focusing on the output: 'I want to make £100k a month' or 'I'll be happy when I hit 20k followers'. But this is the wrong thing to concentrate on. (Followers are *always* the wrong thing to focus on, by the way.)

If £100k is your target, *don't* obsess over the £100k. Obsess over the things that are going to get you there: the **inputs**.

So, if you sell a £5k product and you close one in three people, that means you need to have 60 meetings to get to £100k.

If you have a conversation-to-meeting ratio of 1:5, meaning you have to send five messages to book one meeting, which means you need to have 300 conversations to get those 60 meetings.

300 conversations → 60 meetings → 1:3 close rate → 20 sales → £100k

People *think* they want more sales, of course, they do. That's what brings the money.

**But it's the *leads* that'll get you there: the *inputs*.**

So what inputs do you need be aware of to engineer success?

This is probably where you want to use a client database or spreadsheet to track your data. Start tracking who you talk to, when you talk to them and how you connect.

To keep things simple, here are a few things I recommend tracking:

## Audience data

**Name** → Name of the prospect.
**Email/URL** → Some form of contact info.

**Source** → Where they came from - Email, inbound, outbound, etc.

**Stage** → Nurturing, link sent, call booked, follow-up, etc.

But that's not all. The following are some examples of the key performance indicators (KPIs) or inputs you should *obsess* over.

## Key performance indicator (KPI) data

**Messages sent** → How many messages did you send that day?

**Calls suggested** → How many people did you suggest calls to?

**Links sent** → How many calendar links did you send out?

**Calls booked** → How many sales calls did you book?

**Calls attended** → How many people showed up to the calls?

**Clients won** → How many clients, and how much £££ won?

Once you have three to six months of solid data, you can work out what you need to improve, plus how many messages it takes you to send a link, book a call, convert a client, etc.

This data will tell you if you should charge more, if you need to get a VA or if you aren't doing enough.

**You can see where your strengths and weaknesses lie, and then make a decision that won't come from an emotional place. It'll be a logic-driven decision.**

## The reality of lead generation

Make sure you put time in your diary for this work. Especially at the beginning.

In an ideal world, you'd be spending more than 50% of your working day focused on leads and sales.

It all takes reps. Lots of 'em.

| Mon | Tue | Wed | Thu | Fri |
|---|---|---|---|---|
| Leads & Sales | Other shit | Other shit | Leads & Sales | Other shit |
| Other shit | Leads & Sales | Leads & Sales | Other shit | Leads & Sales |
|  | Other shit |  |  | Other shit |

You could have been doing this for 10 years inconsistently, only taking two sales calls a week, and still not be as skilled as the person with one year's experience who takes 50 calls a week.

Daily repetition is the ultimate aim here.

The more reps you can put into this, the more you'll get these:

- **Visibility**
- **Leads**
- **Sales**

However, don't overdo it and don't over exert yourself.

Consistent and sustainable input is so much better than sporadic, random work. Rather than hitting the workflow like a mad person and sending 200 messages one day, 30 the next and none the next, keep things steady and find the balance that works for you.

You still want to hit those high numbers. This is about volume and consistency, but work your way up.

The best chef in the world could open a restaurant, but that doesn't mean they're going to be booked out and have all the tables filled every single day. That's not a reflection of their talent in the kitchen.

**It's a reflection of their ability to generate attention and capitalise on it.**

*But they're a chef,* you might think, *they're not a businessperson or a marketer.*

And you're right.

**However, relying on your specialism alone is a really big mistake.**

You're a business owner, an entrepreneur or whatever you want to call yourself – so start acting like one!

**Your marketing is what makes a difference in your client attraction.**

My advice to you is to approach lead generation with the mindset of a professional athlete. You're going to face setbacks, failures and lots of rejection along the way. Get used to it. Be willing to put in the hard work and to be resilient when things go against you.

Generating leads for your business is *your* choice.

If you ignore it, you're not going to get any, and someone else will come along and fucking take what's yours.

### MISTAKES TO AVOID

- ✗ Wasting time on people who aren't the right fit.
- ✗ Building a shit lead magnet in 20 minutes (seriously).
- ✗ Stopping lead-generating activities once you see results.
- ✗ Worrying if you don't get a response after sending your first 20 messages.

### ACTIONS TO TAKE NEXT

- ✓ Create your first OTA.
- ✓ Implement the 4C workflow.
- ✓ Send outbound DMs to warm prospects.
- ✓ Put time in your calendar (daily) for leads and sales.
- ✓ Track your data, then revise and improve your process.

# 12 High-Converting posts

**Free Download**

Download my 12 highest converting posts by scanning the following QR code:

**Twelve Posts**

Or by visiting chris-james.co/book-12-posts

# SELL 3

*You've survived every single 'no' people have told you so far.*

# A Brief Intermission:
# Sales Psychology

The ability to sell isn't a skill you're born with.

Everyone thinks slick talkers and killer salespeople are 'naturals', but they're only 'naturals' because they've failed.

Failed again.

And again.

And again.

Tested.

Then perfected.

I was awful to begin with.

Working at that call centre, I'd pray the person I was cold calling wouldn't pick up my call, just so the top performers sitting near me wouldn't hear how shit I was compared to them. I felt like an imposter – and that's because I was.

I hadn't sold a thing in my life.

But sitting near them was a blessing too: I'd listen to their calls, steal the best bits and tweak it into my own cheeky style.

Overcoming the fear was vital; if you didn't hit your numbers, you'd get fired. It's the same with your business: if you don't sell, you'll go bankrupt.

So, like it or not, *selling is essential*.

And it's not as hard as people make out. It's just a sequence of parts that work together to achieve an outcome.

I'll show you what they are in the next three chapters.

## Breaking beliefs

In my opinion, the definition of a successful sales call is helping someone reach the right decision.

But in order to do that, there are often two sets of beliefs that have to change:

1. Your beliefs
2. The buyer's beliefs

### Your beliefs

Your prospect is on the call for a reason – they want help. So they know a pitch is coming. They're not just fishing around; they're likely speaking to you because they hope you're the person who can offer them what they need.

**The most important thing to believe in, more than anything else, is yourself and what you're selling.**

If you have confidence in your offer and you know you can deliver a result, then it's your *duty* to sell to the prospect.

And when I say 'duty', I mean it. You have an obligation.

If you know you can genuinely help this person or their business, you're doing them a *disservice* if you *don't* sell to them. And if that means money exchanges hands, then that's fine.

But the less people believe in themselves, the less likely they're able to sell successfully. When we have self-belief, we display confidence, which is attractive – and *that* will result in more sales.

*Confidence and self-belief come from experience.*

Getting the reps in, seeing the results, and speaking about your offer and business in different situations will give you the experience – and proof – you require to speak confidently, and with conviction.

So, just like DMs, treat sales calls as what they are: just another conversation.

Think about it – the worst thing that can happen is that they say no.

Two little letters.

And you've survived every single no people have told you so far.

A few more won't hurt.

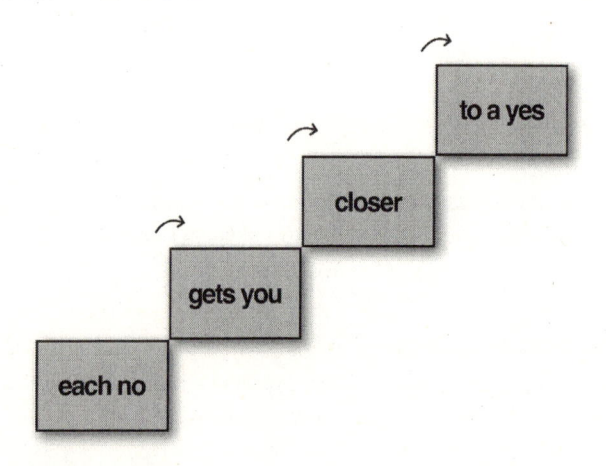

*[Diagram: staircase with boxes labeled "each no" → "gets you" → "closer" → "to a yes"]*

## The buyer's beliefs

Most buyers come to a sales call with a set of beliefs.

In order for them to buy, they must believe these things:

- → They've got a problem they can't solve themselves.
- → There are negative consequences further down the line if they don't fix it.
- → There's a positive pay-off if they solve the problem.
- → Solving the problem is achievable.
- → They can access the finances to fix it.
- → The people around them are going to support their decision to fix it.
- → The way *you* do things is the right solution for the problem.

If, for some reason, they don't believe these things, they'll probably object to the sale.

During the call, we'll work on making sure these beliefs are instilled into the buyer.

So where do you start?

## The new way to sell: Permission-based sales

Let's look at the old way of selling…

It's always the used-car salesman that we think of, right? You express maybe a tiny bit of interest or maybe even no interest at all, and that salesperson becomes as pushy as hell – ramming suggestions, discounts and incentives down your throat.

And then typically they turn cold and weird when you decline.

As a result of these slimeballs, the general public has this old-fashioned misconception about sales.

**The thing is that people *do* like to buy things, but no one likes to think they've been sold to.**

And there's a big difference.

Remember when your parents told you *not* to do something, and you probably went and did it anyway? Just because you don't like being told what to do.

Prospects are the same.

**If you want to convince someone to do something,** *let them think it's their idea.*

When my daughter's getting ready for bed, rather than saying, 'Ivy, get ready for bed,' we say, 'It's bedtime! Do you want to do your teeth first or do you want to get your pyjamas on?'

Ultimately, she gets the choice, but both options are beneficial for us. Both move us closer to the 'conversion' (I guess you could call that permission-based parenting too).

Permission-based sales is very similar. It's a very structured sales process. Instead of seeming too focused on moving forwards, *you're asking for permission to move to the next stage* in a very intentional way.

You typically do that by asking a question that requests their permission:

- → 'How does that sound?'
- → 'Is there anything we've left out?'
- → 'May I ask a question before we move on?'

You're still controlling the call/meeting, but this way, no one feels like they're being pushed anywhere. It's a very non-sleazy, natural progression from saying hello, to finding out more information and then to pitching your solution.

Plus, it gives the prospect the sense of control, which helps them trust you more too.

## The seven-step sales call

If you go to the gym without a plan, you'll probably end up just messing around on a couple of machines, doing a bit of cardio, and maybe going for a swim or a sauna.

After a few weeks, you might begin to wonder why you aren't getting any results.

**Here's why: you need structure to see results.**

Running a sales call without a solid framework is exactly the same. It's easy to go off on tangents and waste time by talking about irrelevant things.

I've found that organising a sales call into the following seven parts removes a lot of the guesswork. It helps you keep control of the call and get the outcomes you want.

What I'm going to show you has been tried and tested through my experiences, and then constantly refined along the way. I use this structure in my business, and it's landed me hundreds of clients and (hopefully, by the time this book is published) seven figures in revenue.

1. Intro
2. Discovery
3. Transition
4. Pitch
5. Tie-down
6. Objections/questions
7. Payment

Over the next three chapters, you're going to learn how to put it into action.

(There's also a link to download my completely free sales call roadmap towards the end of the book as well).

**A few things to remember...**

You're the expert.

And the prospect is interested in speaking to you.

Lead the way and assert yourself from the start.

This is *permission-based* sales, so after every section, ask for 'permission' to move on. It's up to you how to phrase it, but always signal that you're moving on, and make sure they agree and are happy to continue.

**Important:** Never, never skip the discovery phase. It's the most important part of the call, so we'll cover this in-depth next.

# Chapter 7
# Discovery

The other day, my stepson came home with a load of ink on his hands and all over his school blazer.

When I asked him about it, he sheepishly said, 'It's not ink; it's paint.'

*Right. I know what ink looks like.* 'And how did you get it all over your blazer?'

'Freddie knocked it over.'

'So why is it all over *your* hands and face?'

**Sometimes people don't give you all the information.**

They'll often answer without thinking because they're conditioned to or don't feel comfortable telling the truth.

It's like when you ask someone how they are, and they automatically say, 'Not bad,' without stopping to think.

They might not be fine, but we're all conditioned to say we are when asked that question. It's not until you break the pattern and ask, 'No, really, how are you? What's going on?' that they begin to open up.

This is the approach you need to take with your discovery: go a level deeper to understand more about your prospect.

**Sometimes, that will mean asking hard questions.**

In order to help your prospect reach the right decision, you have to look at *where they believe they are now* and *what they need to believe to buy*.

Think of the discovery part of the call as the time to *get to know* your prospect. It's the time to diagnose their problem and find opportunities for you to help.

The reason this part comes so early on is so you can meet them where they are – before you do any pitching.

***It's the questions you* don't *ask that ruin a sale.***

**Everyone comes to sales calls with baggage.**

You might've had a crap call ten minutes ago. Maybe your prospect has been burned by someone in the past or perhaps they've *just* lost their job. (I once sold to a person who had been made redundant 30 minutes before our sales call.)

This baggage enters the call on both sides and affects both your beliefs about each other.

**No one ever knows what the *other* person is bringing to the call, so always go in with an open mind and ask lots of questions.**

Don't shy away from getting to the truth, because the more pain you uncover, the more you can help.

And to do that successfully, there are few things I want to share with you.

## You're not selling

First, let's reframe the concept of a sales call as *an opportunity to help, not to sell*.

Think of this call as a form of coaching. View it as this: 'I'm going to *help* solve this person's problem, and if I'm part of the solution to that problem, then it's a bonus.'

If you're not, then you can still point them in the right direction.

Approaching a sales call from a position of helping will make it feel a lot less transactional.

Think of it as doing your due diligence. *You* are the expert, and it's on you to make sure you're a good fit to help. If you aren't, chances are that the person in front you will end up being a pain-in-the-arse (PITA) client.

This shift from selling to helping will take time and experience, so as with everything else – get your reps in.

## PRO TIP: THE 80%

Based on my experience, about 10% of people who get on a call with you are never going to buy in the first place. There's nothing you can say or do to convince them otherwise. They'll either be a bad fit or they'll just be tyre kickers. (A lot of the time when these people don't buy, it's usually a blessing. Congratulations – you dodged a bullet.)

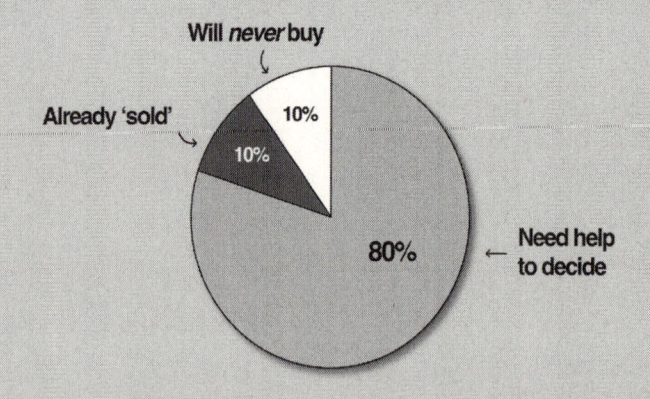

*Will never buy* — 10%
*Already 'sold'* — 10%
*Need help to decide* — 80%

Then there's another 10% who are already sold on your offer, and they're happy to go ahead. They like you because of your marketing, and they're just hopping on a call to sign up or check you're actually a real person.

And then the majority, about 80% of people, need help deciding.

This is where a good discovery phase and asking the right questions is essential; we're breaking beliefs and helping people see that you have the solution.

# Ask the right questions

The first step in helping your prospect solve their problem is getting *them* to admit there is one.

You do that by asking the right questions.

But rather than firing off questions like a robot, it pays to be extremely intentional with *what* and *how* you ask them.

Different types of questions will determine which direction you go in and the information you uncover.

## Open-ended questions

Open-ended questions should be used when you want people to expand and share more details. These are questions that can't be answered with a simple yes or no (unless you're dealing with a teenager), and they usually require a longer answer.

They usually start with one of these words: who, what, where, when or why.

## Closed-ended questions

Closed-ended questions should be used if you want a yes or no answer. Or if you want closure on a topic.

They usually start with one of these words: should, would, can/may, will or do.

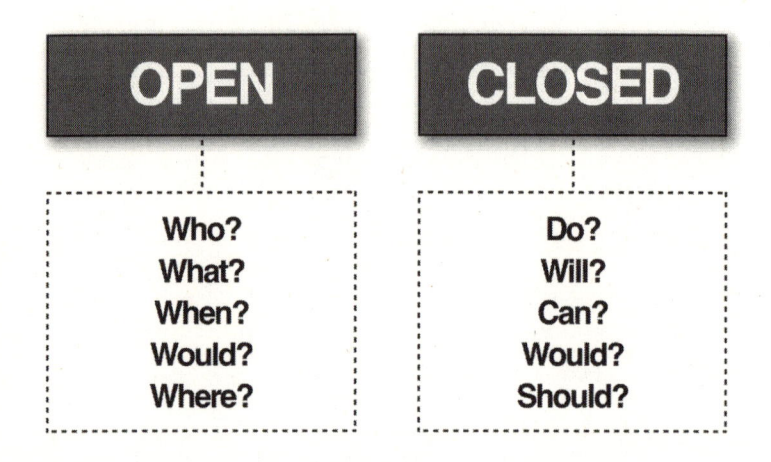

| OPEN | CLOSED |
|---|---|
| Who?<br>What?<br>When?<br>Would?<br>Where? | Do?<br>Will?<br>Can?<br>Would?<br>Should? |

Adapt the questions to the person in front of you. You're not going to ask the same questions to a fitness coach as you would to the owner of an international fintech company. But the process of using open- and closed-ended questions remains the same regardless.

If they say something that could reveal something important, dig deeper. Pair open- and closed-ended questions together to make a bigger impact:

- → **Do** you make less than £2k a month? (Closed)
- → Okay, **how** does that make you feel? (Open)
- → **Why** do you think 48-hour delivery is so important to you? (Open)
- → **Would** you be happier if it was cut down to 24 hours? (Closed)

- → **Are** over 80% of the HR department certified in XYZ? (Closed)
- → **How** does that affect employee happiness? (Open)

Lots of these online 'experts' often advise to only ask open-ended questions in sales scenarios, but that's a load of bollocks. If you want a straight answer, a closed-ended question is the best way to get it.

It depends on the information you're looking to uncover.

## Needs vs wants

If you're *certain* that you can help someone, but they can't necessarily see it, you have to sell them *what they think they want*.

By doing that, you can give them what they *need*.

Last year, my daughter needed to take some awful-tasting medicine. She hated it, and being as stubborn as she is, she refused.

*But she needed it.*

However, in her eyes, the need wasn't worth the discomfort. The pay-off wasn't enough. So we mixed the medicine into her favourite yoghurt and made sure she had a yoghurt every day.

She got the medicine she *needed*, but also the yoghurt she *wanted*.

If you're certain you can help your prospect to achieve their goal, find a way to wrap what they need inside something they want.

If I wanted to lose a load of weight, I'd probably get told I need to go to the gym five days a week, cut out all my favourite foods, track my calories and go for runs – I might not buy that.

It doesn't sound easy or fun.

But I might *want* to buy a '12-week bulletproof programme' that promises I can eat what I want and still lose weight.

> ***Sell people what they want so you can give them what they need.***

> If you're assuming the role of a business owner, that means you're assuming the role of a problem-solver. It's your duty to help people. Don't forget why you're doing this.

## The discovery phase

Now you understand the thinking behind the discovery phase, it's time to put it into action.

The discovery stage of the call or meeting is where you should spend most of your time asking questions and listening to responses.

You have two ears and one mouth for a reason.

Most buyers don't want to be pitched to straight away, but what usually happens is the salesperson will only ask a few questions…

… and then hop straight into selling.

You wouldn't like it if you went into a doctor's office and said, 'I'm in pain,' and they responded, 'Right, we're going to have to amputate your arm,' when all you had was a headache.

That's a bit far-fetched, I know, but think about it…

You can't diagnose someone and prescribe a solution if you don't know what their symptoms are first. And that's the whole point of doing the discovery.

> ***First, seek to understand,***
> ***and then seek to be understood.***

> The negative beliefs we referred to earlier – the ones that can prevent you from getting a sale – won't get broken until you change *someone's* thinking.
>
> So never skip the discovery part of the call.

There are two parts to discovery:

1. The prospect's current situation
2. Their desired situation

## 1. Understand their current situation

The first step of discovery is uncovering the potential buyer's *current* situation. Find out the following:

- → What's their motivation for getting on a call?
- → Where are they right now in life/business?
- → What problem(s) are they looking to solve?
- → What solutions have they already tried?

The prospect must believe they have a problem that's stopping them from getting what they want, so we must ask questions that allow us to uncover the problem at a high level.

Find out what didn't work before and what they've tried and failed with. This knowledge will allow you to pitch more heavily on the things you do differently – and better.

You may have some calls where it might be better to skim over some topics. On others, you'll need to dig deeper. But the ultimate goal for the discovery phase on all calls is to find the *negative* implications of not taking action fast.

**Find the problem and start digging.**

Remember that you're the 'coach.' Ask those deeper questions to unearth more pain. This is where open-ended questions will work really well, such as these: How long has this been going on for? What have you done to try to fix it? Why do you think it didn't work?

*Future pain*

You can then press on their future pain here by asking them this:

- → What will happen if this continues?
- → What if nothing changes?
- → What are the negative consequences of not fixing this problem?

Press on the cost of *not acting now* so as to eliminate time objections and create urgency. Help them believe that standing still is more painful than investing in you.

*Reputation*

Everyone wants to be seen to have made good decisions.

So ask them who they're supported by in this decision; it might be friends, colleagues or family. Understanding that other people could influence their decision to work with you may be an obstacle in closing the sale.

So gather that info too. You might need it later.

## 2. Understand their desired situation

Once you understand where they're at, find out where they want to get to:

- → What's the goal?
- → How quickly do you want to get there?
- → How will you judge the success of working together?

Find out more about their desires, and then help them see the vision of what it would be like to achieve them.

If someone says to me, 'Oh, I just want to get £5k per month,' I'll sometimes push on that and say, 'Only £5k? Why so small?' I'll say it half as a joke, but it gives them permission to dream bigger and articulate their larger goal on the call.

Let them shoot for the stars.

### PRO TIP: BE BRAVE

Your prospect has *chosen* to put themselves on this sales call. They need an expert's help.

So get extremely clear on what's going on in their head and don't be afraid to ask the tough questions.

When people don't close, a lot of the time it's because the discovery part of the call isn't being done properly.

## Widening the gap

Business is about solving problems. When you solve a problem for someone, you create value. And when you create value, people will pay for it.

**More value = more money**

However, it's important to build and sell that picture of the value you offer first. Because when it comes to financial investment, it has to be obvious that investing in *you* is worth it.

So you need to create and widen the gap between their *current* situation and their *desired* situation. Make the current situation feel worse and the desired situation feel more beneficial.

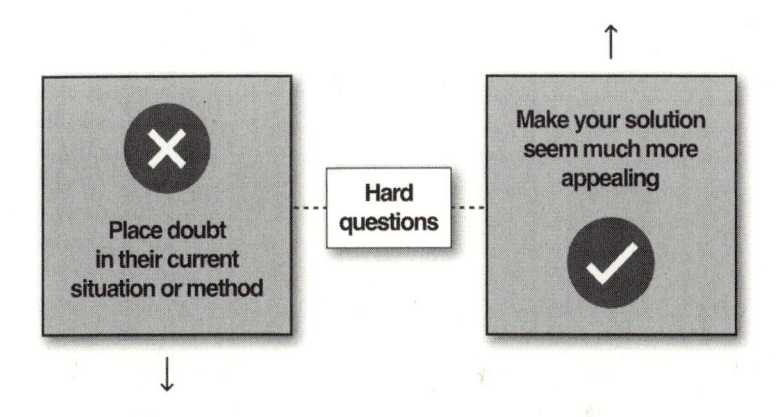

[Diagram: "Place doubt in their current situation or method" (✗) — Hard questions — "Make your solution seem much more appealing" (✓)]

The bigger the gap, the more opportunity there is for you to sell to them.

**So don't feel uncomfortable asking these hard questions.**

After you've gathered all the information, we can transition.

## The transition

This part of the call will help you move to the pitch without feeling pushy, and it consists of the ego boost and the recap.

### The ego boost

This is my favourite part of every sales call.

After you've finished building a vision of the prospect's desired future, pause and compliment them.

You do that by asking questions that might, in this case, work against you.

It sounds counterintuitive, but bear with me…

If they're intelligent, capable and have a wealth of experience, bring that up here. This makes them feel good, and it shows them you're not desperate for their business.

But then, pull back.

'You're clearly very switched on. You've got a successful business and the right team to support you… Why can't you do this on your own?'

Or 'You mentioned you've done XYZ successfully before, so what makes you think you need my help?'

And then be quiet.

Wait.

It's like teasing someone and saying, 'You can have this sweet if you want, but I don't think you'll like it.'

It subconsciously builds desire for what you offer.

**And whatever their answer is will usually be the reason they buy – or go it alone and fail.**

Listen, when people hop on a call with you, they'll already know you offer coaching, consulting, copywriting or whatever it is you do. And the reason they want help will probably be down to one of these:

- **S**peed
- **A**ccountability
- **D**irection

These are also known as the 'SAD reasons'.

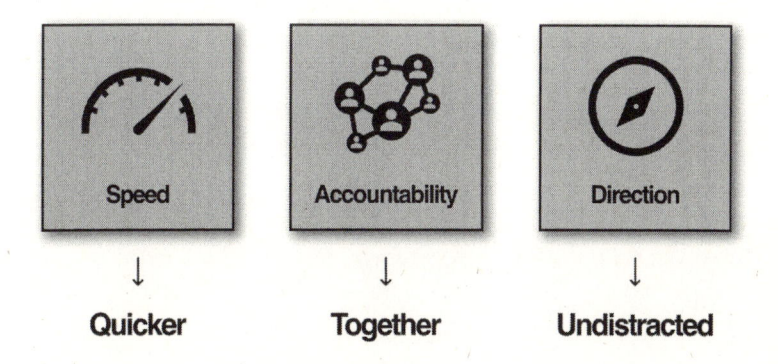

| Speed | Accountability | Direction |
|---|---|---|
| ↓ | ↓ | ↓ |
| **Quicker** | **Together** | **Undistracted** |

They'll want to buy a quicker outcome, have more support or follow a proven process that eliminates all the guesswork. Listen carefully to their answer and write it down. What they say here could be vital ammo for later in the objections phase.

## Recap

The recap is your indicator that the pitch is coming.

Summarise the discussion so far:

- → 'Your current situation is XYZ.'
- → 'And you want to get to ABC.'
- → 'What's standing in your way is 123.'
- → 'You've mentioned you need help with speed/accountability/direction [or a mixture of all three].'

And then ask them to confirm it: 'Does that sound right?'

Getting them to confirm creates a subconscious signal to themselves that they're happy to move to the next stage. It also shows that you've listened to and understood them.

If they say it's not right or your solution isn't a good fit, ask a few more questions and be prepared to dance around a little bit. (Hopefully, you've done most of the dancing in the discovery phase.)

Then ask, 'Is there anything else you feel I need to know?'

Most of the time, they'll say no, and that's your cue to close this part of the call and move to the pitch.

If they say yes, then it's probably something you want to hear, so go back into discovery mode and unpick their answer further.

If there's nothing else, you can ask permission to pitch: 'The good news is I can definitely help. Would you like me to show you what my solution looks like?'

They give you permission…

… and then you move to the pitch.

## MISTAKES TO AVOID

- ✗ Rushing.
- ✗ Losing control of the call.
- ✗ Not listening to their responses.
- ✗ Skipping over questions to get to the pitch.

## ACTIONS TO TAKE NEXT

- ✓ Practise asking your questions.
- ✓ Fine-tune your technique continuously.
- ✓ If you're doing these calls remotely, always hit 'record' (if you have that option).
- ✓ Be mindful of whether your questions are open- or closed-ended.

*Don't start a business if you're scared of asking people to buy your shit.*

# Chapter 8
# Pitch

**Anyone can pitch.**

But to pitch effectively is a skill. It's saying the right words, in the right way and in the right order. It's using the right tone, with the right pauses and the right facial expressions.

Follow the structure I'm going to show you. If you do, you'll have a pitch that's clear, organised and positions you as the answer to your prospect's problem.

> ***Don't start a business if you're scared of asking people to buy your shit.***

You can do all the marketing and content in the world, but none of it matters if you're scared of selling. So you, my friend, are gonna have to fucking suck it up.

Now, you might be very lucky and have a massive audience. Maybe you're able to get a load of web traffic through to your site and sell a product on a click-to-buy basis.

But the people I work with are service-based business owners. That means their clients usually require a human touch to buy.

As the business owner (especially in the early stages of your business), you're pretty much the only human qualified to do that.

No matter what you believe about your sales skills, *you* are the only one capable of pitching your solution in the best way. (At least until you can scale up and train up a team, but that's another book.)

But…

**… expect things to go wrong.**

If I asked you to drive a car, but you've never driven before, you're going to stall and mess up.

You might crash.

You might reverse into your own house, like I did (and that was after I passed my driving test.)

Success in sales is about *repeated* exposure to sales scenarios.

And that means repeated exposure to *uncomfortable* and *messy* situations.

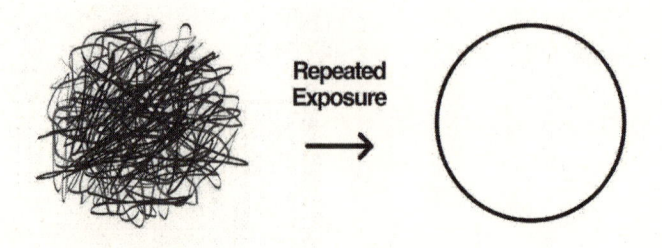

Obviously, you're going to feel apprehensive; you're going to a place you've never been before.

But as we've touched on, if you want to stay in that comfort zone, you can. Just don't pitch, don't convert – and don't make any sales.

**You're reading this book for a reason.**

I'm guessing it's because you want to make more money, or at least get more clients who pay you money.

And the only way to do both of those things is to be able to convert.

This is how you do it…

## Life's a pitch

> If you skipped ahead to this chapter and did none of the earlier work, you need to go back to *Chapter 1* and do it. Stop trying to cut corners.

This is where all the groundwork we've already laid in the book will come together.

You know what your promise, phases and parts are.

You know your message.

You've done the traction exercise, and you have feedback.

You know what your market wants.

You have leads or people who are interested in your solution.

The pitch is where you'll present your solution, based on the information you've gathered in the discovery phase.

After you do 30 or so of these sales calls, you'll start to notice patterns. The people you speak to will tend to say the same things. Use that data to adapt this sales call structure to your style.

### PRO TIP: WARNING

You can't pitch without doing the discovery. If you haven't got the information, your pitch will be off because you'll be guessing.

You might waste time talking about stuff that's not relevant, or you may pitch something the buyer doesn't want or need.

**So, for the love of God, please conduct a proper discovery *before* the pitch.**

## Step 1. Promise: The outcome

Start your pitch by reiterating your promise: the outcome/results your clients get from working with you.

'As you might know, I work with [audience] to help them achieve [outcome]…'

Refer back to the work you did on your promise in *Chapter 1*.

## Step 2. Phases: The major milestones

Any sophisticated buyer isn't going to care if they get 1m hours' worth of course material and 64 one-to-one coaching sessions with you. All they care about is that there's a very clear path to success and that path is relevant to them.

**They want to know about the transformation, the results you provide and how long it takes.**

So you want to talk about the phases next.

When explaining each phase, don't describe every single thing that's involved, even if there are 47 steps in each phase. They'll get confused and stop listening.

Be clear and tell them how each phase helps them to achieve their outcome.

I recommend preparing what you're going to say using the following technique. It might not be relevant to every phase, but you can adapt this to your offer, your style and what your prospect needs to hear. Don't get hung up on sticking to these six sections when describing every phase, or your pitch could end up sounding very scripted.

This is simply a recommended structure for you to adapt to your style. However, I've found that this is the best way to break any negative beliefs and install new, empowering beliefs in your prospect.

Test it out and find what works for you.

## 1. Direction

Firstly, describe the phase in a way that gives your prospect direction and shows you're the expert. Use assumptive language that helps them to visualise working together:

- → 'So, the very first thing we're going to do is…'
- → 'In the second phase, we'll…'
- → 'Once we've completed this, the final phase will…'

## 2. Mistakes

Then attack the wider mistakes people tend to make in this area:

- → 'So, you told me that you have trouble with XYZ, and that's because you don't ABC…'
- → 'Most people make the mistake of rushing in without planning…'
- → 'I know a lot of people in your position think they have to XYZ…'

## 3. Negative consequences

Be sure to explain the negative consequences of that mistake:

- → '… and because of that they never get any leads.'
- → '… but that usually means they never get anywhere.'
- → '… and that's why most people fail to achieve their goal.'

## 4. Your solution

Position yourself as the answer and offer your alternative:

→ 'So that's why we're going to XYZ instead...'

## 5. Positive consequence

Emphasise the positive consequence:

→ '... because you can perform better / people will book calls / you'll win more clients.'

I've just given you a lot of information, so to help you, let's look at an example of what that might look like when it's put together:

**1** → **Direction**

**2** → **Mistakes**

**3** → **Negative Consequences**

**4** → **Solution**

**5** → **Positive Consequences**

*Example pitch*

**1. Direction:** 'So, the *very first* thing we're *going* to do is create a tailored nutrition and lifestyle plan for you.'

**2. Mistakes:** 'Most personal trainers *make the mistake* of rushing their clients into a generic training regime. They don't consider what fuel the body needs to be able to perform at its best.'

**3. Negative consequences:** '*And because of that*, workouts don't have their full effect. Clients tend to perform well for the first couple of weeks, then they plateau or fall off very quickly.'

**4. Solution:** 'So, *instead*, we'll get extremely clear on your sleep, water intake, food preferences and schedule. There's no point asking you to do things you dislike or that don't fit in with your existing commitments, which is why we start with the plan itself.'

**5. Positive consequences:** 'Doing this first is going to result in you showing up with more energy and getting results faster. You'll be filled with confidence on your wedding day and also maintain a sustainable approach for months to come.'

> **PRO TIP: ADAPT TO YOUR PROSPECT**
>
> Tailor the phases to the needs of your prospect.
>
> If they've mentioned they're struggling with productivity, and your phase 2 is built specifically to solve this, spend more time explaining phase 2 and less time on 1 and 3.
>
> Pull out elements of your offer that relate to your prospect's situation.

## 6. Sense check

The aim of this is to remove any of their baggage before talking about price.

Once you've run through your phases, double-check that the prospect is clear on your process and that they're bought in. If they're not, you might have a problem.

Say something like this: 'Before I go into the nuts and bolts [signalling that you're coming to the end of this section], does that process sound like it's going to help? Is that the kind of thing you're looking for?'

Use closed-ended questions: you want that yes (or no).

At this point, lots of prospects will jump in and start asking about the deliverables.

But it's your job here to pull back and keep control of the call: 'I'll go through the nuts and bolts in a sec; I just want to make sure you're super clear on the process itself. What questions do you have?'

This gives you permission to move to the next stage and helps the prospect confirm to themselves that the process works for them.

It also helps you address any concerns they might have with the process.

## PRO TIP: VISUAL AIDS

Help people picture success. Literally.

Use visual aids in your pitch to give a glimpse of what it's like to work with you.

I'm not talking about a whole slide show, but remember that a picture is worth a thousand words – and that could be a digital whiteboard you draw diagrams on, a document that displays the process, or perhaps an illustrated roadmap or a quick look at some client results…

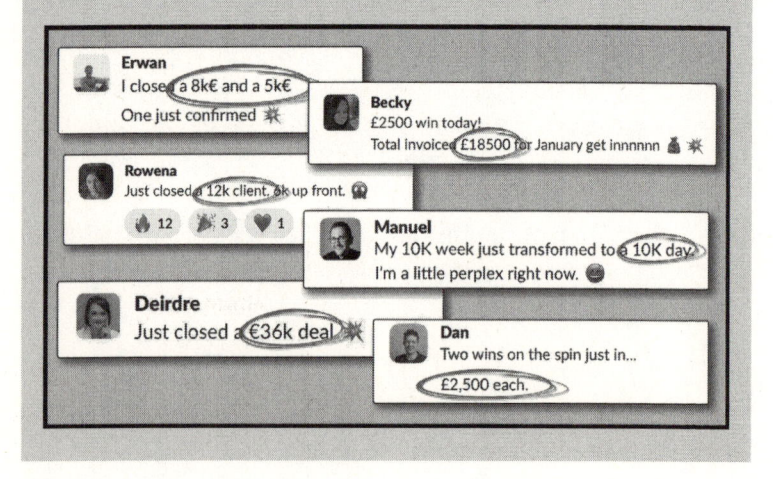

> **Erwan**
> I closed a 8k€ and a 5k€
> One just confirmed 💥
>
> **Becky**
> £2500 win today!
> Total invoiced £18500 for January get innnnnn 💰 💥
>
> **Rowena**
> Just closed a 12k client, 6k up front. 😮
> 👍 12  🎉 3  ❤ 1
>
> **Manuel**
> My 10K week just transformed to a 10K day
> I'm a little perplex right now. 😅
>
> **Deirdre**
> Just closed a €36k deal 💥
>
> **Dan**
> Two wins on the spin just in…
> £2,500 each.

## Step 3. Parts: Deliverables

This is the final part of the pitch in which you should talk about your deliverables: the nuts and bolts of your offer.

A big mistake people make here is to go into far too much detail. If the prospect is bought into you and your process, there's no need to oversell.

If you've followed the structure correctly, the buyer should be satisfied that you can help solve their problem. Now it's just a question of literally rattling these off:

- → The main element you offer
- → The resources and support they get
- → The tools they get access to
- → The bonuses (if any)

But run it through the marketer's lens again and spice up the parts:

- → They don't just get access to a community; they get access to 'An exclusive community full of people on the same journey as you.'
- → There's not just reporting; they get 'Detailed analytics delivered once a week so we can track progress and address any concerns instantly.'
- → It's not email support; it's 'Access to me throughout the whole process through email or WhatsApp, so we can problem solve in real time.'

**That's much more powerful.**

You should have done this work in *Chapter 1*, but if you haven't, please go back and do it.

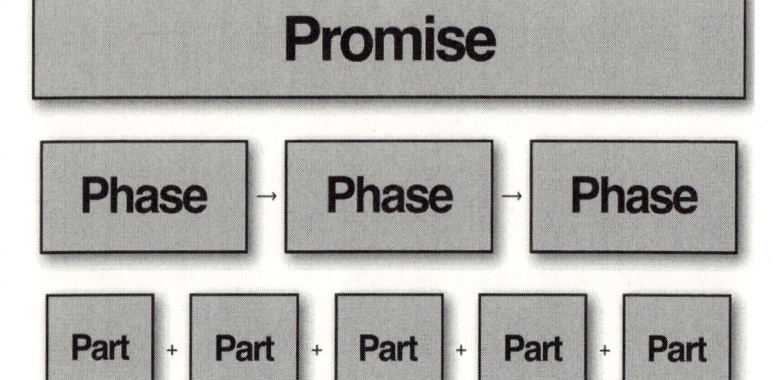

```
┌─────────────────────────────┐
│          Promise            │
└─────────────────────────────┘

[Phase] → [Phase] → [Phase]

[Part] + [Part] + [Part] + [Part] + [Part]
```

> ### PRO TIP: AUTHENTICITY
>
> There's something special and more authentic about sharing things in real time.
>
> I've done calls where I've just screen-shared our community wins inside the C2C Slack channel. I tell the prospect they're reading client results from today or the last 48 hours, and then I read off some wins.
>
> Be resourceful.
>
> If you don't have a Slack channel brimming with results, what else have you got?

> Can you share WhatsApp messages from clients or emails you can screenshot? Can you put them together in a Google Doc? (That's an OTA.)
>
> Like I say, this isn't to be confused with a full 45-minute slide show or death by PowerPoint.
>
> It's about giving them little glimpses into what you offer.
>
> If your marketing's good enough, people should already know how happy your clients are, but if not, give them a look behind the scenes.

**Give yourself permission to adapt to the prospect.**

If they ask whether you offer any bonus materials, ask what they had in mind. (You can say yes and build it later.)

If someone suggests you need to do a masterclass on a particular technique, you don't have to tell them it's not built yet.

Sell it first, then as soon as they sign off and pay, go away and build it.

Use this as an opportunity to listen to what your market wants – and then build it for them. It's all about acting on that feedback.

## The tie-down

You don't want to jump straight into talking about price without getting permission first. That's why you need a *transition* into talking about the investment.

This is where the tie-down comes in. This section is made up of the gauge and next steps.

This is about making sure there are no limiting beliefs, worries or red flags left. It'll help the discussion about money feel more natural and less awkward.

**The goal is to leave no unanswered questions before talking money.**

The only thing the prospect should be thinking (and this is the ideal scenario) is this: *If the money's right, I'm in.*

It's a lot easier to handle a money objection when you know the buyer has bought into the process. If you don't push them on this, it'll be on you if the sale doesn't happen, so now is your last chance to check.

### Gauge: What questions do they have?

Acknowledge that you've been talking for the last 5–10 minutes and you've given them a lot of information. Now is a good time to ask what questions they have now they know your process and whether they have any concerns.

If you want to be a bit more forward, you can ask something like this: 'Besides the price, is there anything else that would stop you moving forwards?'

If you have a sense that something's not quite right or they didn't react as positively as you'd hoped, be open and call them out: 'I saw your face when I mentioned XYZ. Let's talk about that for a second. How does that make you *feel*?' (Make sure you emphasise 'feel'.)

**People often aren't anywhere near as assertive as they need to be, so give them permission to be open and honest with you.**

Challenge any sticking points they have.

You should already have an idea of what the points could be from the discovery stage, but these things could still come into play at this stage too.

If they do have concerns, drill down on them.

What part of the process do they think might not work? Have a quick discussion.

Remember, we aren't talking cost – *yet*.

### PRO TIP: MEASURE THEIR FEELINGS

A good way to gauge their feeling is to help them put their thoughts into numbers:

> 'Aside from the cost, on a scale of 0% to 100%, where 0% is "absolutely not" and 100% is "I'm all in", where do you sit?'
>
> If they say 75%, you can ask them what it would take to get to 100%.
>
> Do this in a way that's still light-hearted. Have a smile on your face, lean in and be engaged.

## Next steps: How this works

If they're happy to move on or you've discussed their concerns, you then want to tell the prospect what will happen after you talk price:

- → You're either going to press forwards and onboard them
- → You're going to set up the next call for the close

At this stage, anticipation of the price has been building.

They've probably been waiting to find out about the investment for half an hour, but you still need to tell them what will happen at the end of the call. *Anything* could ruin the sale after the meeting ends: a competitor could approach them, someone could hijack their thinking and change their mind, their spouse could get sick, or they could just forget.

**You don't want them to swan off into the distance after telling them the price; you want to close them then and there, if possible.**

Make a joke of it and acknowledge that the price is coming:

'Before we get to the elephant in the room, I want to talk about what happens next if you're happy to proceed.' (Or whatever way you want to phrase it.)

> ### PRO TIP: THE MULTIPLE-CALL CLOSE
>
> You'll either have a one-call close or a multiple-call close depending on what you sell and the space you're in.
>
> If you need multiple calls to close, then at the very least, now is the time to schedule that second call. That's either to present a proposal or to bring the extra decision-makers in, for example.
>
> In this case, mentioning a ballpark investment typically works quite well, and you'll want to gauge that reaction by asking what they think.
>
> If your business means you have to present a proposal that needs work, use the second call as the time to do it.
>
> I also don't recommend sending proposals via email. Always present them face to face or on a video call. You want to be ready to respond to problems in real time or to discuss the parts of the project with the decision-makers.
>
> Once you've touched on ballpark costs, open up your calendar on the call and set dates.

# Money

## The investment: Price or ballpark figure

Now comes money.

The main thing people fuck up here is saying the price and then immediately trying to justify it.

Don't.

You'll sound desperate.

**Give your prospect time to think.**

Don't talk. Do *not* justify.

Wait.

| Say the price | Shut up | And wait |

Be willing to swim in discomfort for a few seconds. There are a lot of things going on in your prospect's head, especially if this is a one-call close and they're being asked to make a big decision.

The worst thing you can do is to overload them with even more information.

A good technique is to deliberately take a sip of water, pause and remind yourself to relax.

> It's here that they might bring up some objections, and you need to be ready for them. We'll cover objections in the next chapter.

## Incentivise them to take action

The one question you should always ask yourself (and you should already have this figured out before the call) is why potential clients should take action *now*.

It's your job to get them to act as fast as possible because it's in their best interest to solve this problem or reach that goal.

So you should incentivise them to act quickly.

**Give them a reason to act now**

A couple of examples you could use to do this are as follows:

- → Offer them an extra month, call or free resource if they pay now.
- → Offer them a bonus you mentioned as part of the deliverables.
- → Offer them a bonus you made up on the spot.

Scarcity and/or urgency are good to use too:

- → Tell them you only have one slot available.
- → Tell them you're speaking to someone tonight who intends to pay straight away.
- → Tell them if they pay now, they avoid the upcoming price increase.

## Payment

So, you got a yes.

Brilliant.

Now you want to take payment or a deposit as fast as possible.

Whether it's a one-call close or a multiple-call close, if they give you the go-ahead, wherever possible, *take payment or a deposit on the call.*

That means having your bank details, some form of payment processing link or shopping cart ready to copy and paste into the chat or to give them in person.

**You need to capitalise when people are at their hottest.**

If you're ever on a sales call with the C2C team, the minute you give us a yes, our bank details or a Stripe link will be in that Zoom chat in 10 seconds or less.

Don't let people dwell on it.

If you do, they're much less likely to take action.

If you can't take payment right then, get some other form of written or financial commitment before the call ends. An example would be an initial top-level contract.

### PRO TIP: MINDSET

This might feel uncomfortable for you.

After a while, you'll start to see you're missing out on a lot of revenue if you resist asking for that commitment early.

You need to capitalise on when people are *most likely* to buy.

And that means getting comfortable with being uncomfortable.

## Onboarding process

Once you've got written or financial approval, you want to take your new client through your onboarding process.

Unfortunately, this isn't a book about onboarding, and every business will have different processes. Generally, you want to make sure clients have a positive experience.

There's nothing worse than transferring a load of money or agreeing to something with a new supplier, and then not seeing or hearing from them for 10 days.

People want stuff fast.

They want same-day delivery.

Give them something there and then that they can jump into – whether it's a dashboard, materials or even booking their first call with you. I once sent someone a private link to a single lesson from the C2C course after they'd paid their deposit on the call. It was just so they could get started before joining properly.

Get creative if you've not got any assets yet.

But hold on – what if you get a no?

Something got missed. A discussion wasn't had, or they didn't tell you key information. If possible, drill down into what's stopping them. Again, you can learn a lot from the objections chapter coming up next.

## PRO TIP: KNOWING WHEN TO STOP

I only ever press people two or three times if I feel I can really help them.

If I can see they're not going to move forwards, and nothing I say will change their mind, I'm happy to let it go and trust that they'll be back.

I once had someone come back after 12 months. Nothing had changed. He hadn't progressed, but that was something he had to figure out on his own.

It's much better to work with clients who want to work with you than those who are conflicted about it.

Trust yourself and know when to keep pressing and when to walk away.

## MISTAKES TO AVOID

- ✗ Don't make assumptions about your prospect.
- ✗ Saying the price and justifying it immediately.
- ✗ Not taking payment / a deposit on the call.

## ACTIONS TO TAKE NEXT

- ✓ Prepare and practise your pitch.
- ✓ Have tabs open with testimonials, links to your course/portfolio, Slack channel or anything else you think could help on the call.
- ✓ Have your digital whiteboard or a blank Google Doc ready.
- ✓ Have your bank details or payment link to hand so you can copy and paste it the minute you get the go-ahead. (Or have a contract ready.)
- ✓ Record all your sales calls.

# Chapter 9
# Objections

Imagine you're going to spend £1k on a new TV.

Even though you know what you want, you're still going to have questions or need further clarity on something. Can you mount it on the wall? Will it match your speakers? Can it be delivered tomorrow? Can you disable YouTube to stop your kids poisoning their brains with those awful fucking unboxing videos?

If you think about any big decision you've ever made, you'll always have had questions. There's always a reason why you might not spend that money or commit to that thing.

**This is a natural stage of the buying cycle.**

But I still see a lot of business owners getting scared and uptight about this part: the objections.

I'll be honest: I love the objection part of the sale. It's like doing a dance – back and forth, back and forth.

**However, the toughest thing about it is there's no silver bullet for objections**.

Sales trainers make a lot of money claiming 'objection-handling training' will solve all your problems. But all that does is turn objections into some massive mountain of fear you have to overcome – when in reality, it's not.

When someone objects, see it as a sign that they need more clarity.

Maybe they have a couple of extra thoughts they want reassurance on or they still don't fully understand why your solution is going to work for them.

The worst thing you can do is get your back up when they display an objection.

**It's not 'you vs them'.**

You want to challenge their thinking, but don't disagree with them directly in a confrontational way. You're not a *Street Fighter* character trying to beat them into submission.

**You're not trying to win: you both want the same thing.**

This is about having a mindset of empathy and guiding your prospect towards making the right decision – for *them*. Seek to understand their motivations. Find out what beliefs are holding them back at this stage.

In this chapter, instead of giving you scripts, I'm going to give you pointers and frameworks created from a psychological point of view.

There's no one-size-fits-all solution that's going to magically handle every single objection. But once you understand *why* people act the way they do, especially in relation to buying, things will become a lot easier.

> **Disclaimer:**
> What I'm about to share is all based on your prospect being a good fit for your offer. Enlisting the wrong people as clients is just going to come back to bite you in the arse, and honestly, it's just not worth it.
>
> Plus, it's ethically wrong.
>
> They're well within their rights to decline your offer too. But if you know you can help this person, you owe it to them – and yourself – to ask some hard questions during this stage.

## Handling objections

So, at this point, you've done a full discovery, you've pitched your offer correctly and, theoretically, you've addressed all their concerns. If the money's right, the person should buy...

But as we know, that's not always the case – which is why objections occur.

It's important for you to know that they're not a bad thing.

**Objections should be seen as a *positive*.**

If your prospect really wasn't interested, they'd probably end the meeting straight away, or they wouldn't have even taken it in the first place, right?

So *there is interest*, it's just a bump in the road you need to drive over – *together*.

You should view their objection as a signal they don't have a full understanding of your offer. It's therefore your job to guide them towards clarity. It's a bit like coaching: you're just operating in their best interests to help them see the solution.

Reframe it as an opportunity for you to give them more information and help them move closer towards their goal.

## Questions vs objections

An 'objection' can appear as either a statement or a question. You can look at them in the same light, but under the surface, what they reveal about the prospect is very different.

Take the phrase 'It's too expensive' compared to 'Do you offer discounts?'

They both communicate the same issue: the prospect has a money concern. But they both feel different and reveal the state of mind your prospect is in.

**A statement reveals a reason not to buy, but a question is typically a buying signal.**

When dealing with objections, remember it's an *opportunity* for you to move your prospect in the right direction.

I always recommend having an internal filter or interceptor in your head that *reframes* any statements you get into questions.

As an example, if someone asks, 'Can I have a discount?' that's not an objection; that's a **question**. (Obviously.)

It's a really good question too because it displays a high level of interest. You don't need to reframe it, and you can answer it without any issue. It's a yes or no. (In this scenario, say no).

But if someone says, 'XYZ is cheaper,' then that's a **statement**.

It's also a reason for that person *not* to buy. So here's where you reframe it as a question internally: *Why* is XYZ cheaper? *How* did they make it cheaper?

***Important:* You're reframing this all in your head. Don't say this out loud!**

Once you've reframed it as a question, you're in a better position to help change your prospect's thinking:

'Well, yeah, you're right. They are cheaper. But let me ask you this: *why* do you think they're cheaper?'

You'll find some ways to reframe objections later in this chapter.

## Digging deeper

A lot of the time when people bring up objections, their thoughts are distorted and unclear. What they say and think isn't always an accurate reflection of their reality.

Sometimes, that's intentional and is a **conscious concealment**.

And other times, it's *un*intentional, and it's a **subconscious distortion**.

With conscious concealment, the person is hiding their real objection from you on purpose. They might be embarrassed or want to avoid being seen as weak.

When it's a subconscious distortion, it's usually a false belief they hold. A set of lies they're telling themselves or baggage left over from past experiences / other people around them.

If you know you can help them and you know they're the right fit, you need to do everything you can to empower them and the way they think.

So, when they bring up an objection, take a step back and try to understand what the prospect is *really* saying. Just because they say it's too expensive or they don't have time, that doesn't necessarily mean it's the whole truth.

Your job is to find the root cause, and you can do that in a very specific way.

## The three types of objection

This isn't a one-size-fits-all situation.

Some objection exchanges can take two minutes; others can take 20.

When it takes longer, it's usually a sign that there are a number of different layers you need to peel back before you can get to the truth. It's a bit like an onion. Don't jump straight to the core of the problem. People don't usually respond well to that.

This is a process to take carefully: layer by layer and in a specific order.

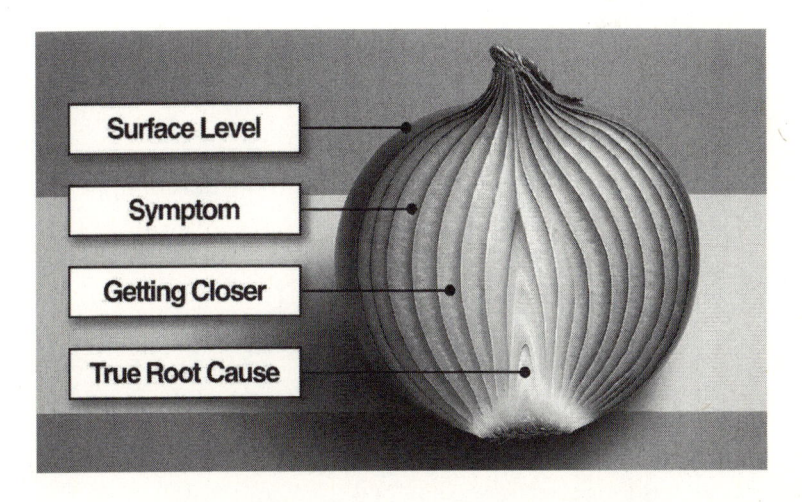

- Surface Level
- Symptom
- Getting Closer
- True Root Cause

*Not all objections are created equal.*
*And not all objections are the truth.*

I've found there are three main blockers or barriers to overcome that stop people from buying:

*1. External factors*

These are some examples of external reasons that may be stopping someone from buying:

- No / not enough money
- Not enough time / the time isn't right
- An element of the process they don't think will work for them

Most objections will start here, but that doesn't mean this is the true reason they might not buy.

*2. Other people*

They need to seek permission or support from, speak to, or feel judged by one of these:

- Their spouse
- Their partner
- A colleague/boss

*3. Internal factors*

These are some examples of internal reasons that may be stopping someone from buying:

- A limiting belief
- Avoidance
- Fear

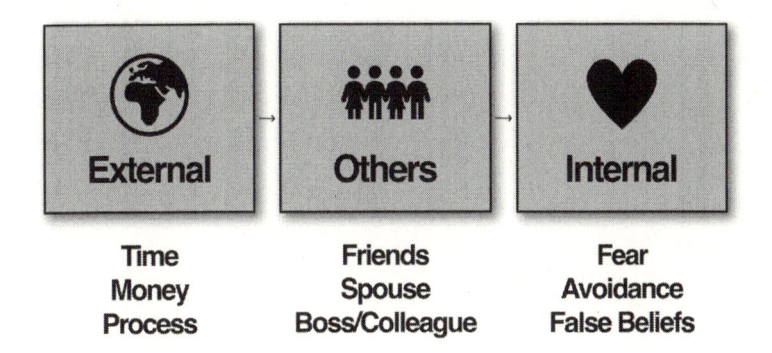

| External | Others | Internal |
|---|---|---|
| Time | Friends | Fear |
| Money | Spouse | Avoidance |
| Process | Boss/Colleague | False Beliefs |

**You may come across every single one of these types in one call, or you might experience only one. And they could appear in any order. Be ready to adapt to the person in front of you.**

Understand that it's at the *internal layer* where the truth lies.

**That's where the real decision is made.**

It's easy for anyone to say they don't have time for something. It's easy to say they can't afford it.

But if I offered someone a £2m mansion for £500 if they paid today, chances are they would find the fucking money. Fast.

They'd do it because it's a no-brainer.

People will find a way to achieve their goals if they truly believe it's within their reach, and they'll find money if they see the value in something.

So, when it comes to the objection stage, you win the sale by reshaping their thinking and helping them believe it *is* possible.

And you do that by peeling back these layers bit by bit, so you can help people see the truth for themselves.

> ### PRO TIP: THE INTERNAL OBJECTION
>
> When you get to those internal objections, this is where the 'coaching' truly begins. There'll be something core that's holding them back, and your role is to help them confront reality.
>
> However, even though your goal will be to get down to their core internal objection, it doesn't mean you should skip over any 'external' or 'other' objections.
>
> At the same time, if a prospect willingly reveals their internal objection, and you can solve it, the first two types of objection almost become irrelevant.
>
> Trust yourself and know when to keep pressing and when to walk away.

So now you know about the three types of objections, what do you do when they come up on the call?

You use the VIPER framework:

| V | I | P | E | R |
|---|---|---|---|---|
| Validate | Isolate | Permission | Expand | Return |

## The VIPER framework

This framework is based on the prospect being the right fit. Perhaps they're so perfect for what you offer you're almost annoyed they can't see it.

I've had calls with people where I'll think, *This is ridiculous; you're absolutely perfect for this programme.* But they're still sitting on the fence, for whatever reason.

It's people like that who you'll have to confront, challenge and push a little bit – maybe a lot – in order to help them.

### Validate

When someone displays an objection, don't get defensive or upset.

Validate it. Make them feel heard.

Find common ground that shows them you understand their situation and can relate. Don't just jump in with questions or challenges. Show them you're on their side:

- → 'That makes sense.'
- → 'I'd do the same.'

## Isolate

Get to the root objection: the biggest thing in their way.

Make sure the objection they're bringing up is the only one and that there aren't any others. This will help eliminate smokescreens – or it'll bring more objections to the table.

Say things such as 'hypothetically', 'for example' and 'let's pretend' to take the pressure off and help them imagine an alternative situation:

- → 'Hypothetically, if XYZ weren't an issue, what else would stop you from going ahead?'
- → 'Let's say ABC were already fixed; would you be ready?'

If nothing else arises, and they agree this is the only thing, then you continue.

If other objections do come up, it may be a case of providing more information or clarifying parts of your offer.

Deal with each of the other objections until you get to the root cause: the *single* objection that your prospect agrees is the *only* thing stopping them from moving forwards.

## Permission

Once you've isolated the objection, ask permission to make a suggestion or ask a further question.

A soft, non-confrontational question will take the sting out of any objection exchange. Again, it gives the prospect the feeling of control, and it changes the dynamic of the conversation. It takes the focus off them and builds anticipation for what you're about to ask:

- → 'Can I make a suggestion?'
- → 'Can I ask you something?'

## Expand

This is the toughest part of handling objections because it's based on shifting someone's thoughts. It's where you reframe their thinking and help them visualise the outcome they want – or don't want. You can think of your job here as rewiring the prospect's brain. We'll explore this fully in the next section of this chapter.

This is truly tailored to them and can't be scripted. Typically, your expansion should highlight something they've already said, which you then reframe:

- → 'You mentioned XYZ. If that happens, what would you do?'
- → 'I remember you said ABC. Would that still be the case if...?'

## Return

Once you feel there's progress or the objection has been handled, loop back and ask for the sale. Don't lose momentum; this is still a sales call, so you want to keep nudging towards the close.

***Important***: This framework won't work for every objection, and you'll have to be flexible enough to adapt to the person in front of you. But use it in your calls and you'll start to see how powerful it is.

## Examples

Let's look at some examples of how you can potentially expand on an objection, reframe it and then overcome it.

This isn't a list of responses to use, but prompts for you to start thinking about how you'd expand on the objections you're likely to get.

---

**Example 1:** 'I need to speak to my spouse.'

---

**V: Validate** → 'Great. That means you're taking this seriously!'

**I: Isolate** → 'Let's say they agreed that this was a good idea. Would there be anything else stopping you from pulling the trigger today?'

**P: Permission** → 'Okay. Do you mind if I ask you a question?'

**E: Expand** → 'Usually, when people run things by their spouse, what's really happening is that they don't want to fail and look stupid – or look like they've made a bad decision... So what makes you think this won't work for you?'

**R: Return** → [This should reveal the real reason. Handle it and continue to ask for the sale.]

---

**Example 2:** 'I need to think about it.'

**V: Validate** → 'That makes sense; it's a big decision.'

**I: Isolate** → 'I've got to ask, though: what is it you need to think about? What is it *specifically* that's stopping you from jumping all over this right now?'

**P: Permission** → 'May I ask a personal question?'

**E: Expand** → 'You've been thinking about this for years. You've come this far and are so close. If you turn back now, do you really want to be in the same position in six months?'

**R: Return** → [Handle the real reason, loop back and ask for the sale.]

## PRO TIP: MINDSET

I've said this before, and I'll say it again: if you can help this person or their business with whatever it is you do, *you fucking owe it to them* to help them.

If you don't ask that extra question to make them explain themselves in the nicest possible way, they might try to go it alone – or buy from someone who isn't as good as you.

And they'll probably fail – and it'll be *your fault*. All because you held back.

They *need your help* if they're a good fit, and it's your job to sell to them.

It might sound like I'm coming across as a bit of a prick, and I know I'm repeating myself, but I want *you* to know how important it is to not give up too easily.

If you genuinely believe you can help someone, you owe it to them, you owe to yourself and you owe it to the world to do just that.

And if it involves taking money off them to do so, that's fine, so long as you're sure you can get them closer to their desired outcome.

## Closing techniques

If all else fails, these three closing techniques work well and are my favourite methods for belief shifting:

- The scenario ladder
- The happiness scale
- The comparison principle

### The scenario ladder

Usually, when people are considering C2C it's because they want knowledge, money or to meet like-minded people. So I play out the potential scenarios for them: from getting no results to getting exponential results.

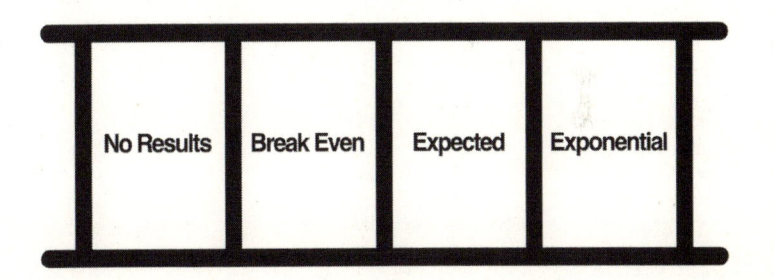

[Ladder diagram with rungs labelled: No Results | Break Even | Expected | Exponential]

The conversation might go like this:

You: 'Okay, you need to think about it, and I get that, but let's walk through all the potential outcomes.

'**Scenario A. No results:** You come in, pay me and get *no* results. You meet *no* people and make *no* money.

'**Scenario B. Break even:** You learn *one* thing, only meet *one* person and *only* make your money back.

'**Scenario C. Expected:** You learn some key principles that are going to last forever. You hit your financial goals, and you meet a bunch of cool people.

'**Scenario D. Exponential:** You completely level up your mindset. You make £1m in the first month, and you turn every single person who looks at you into a client instantly.

'Which do you think is most likely? A, B, C or D?'

Most people will say B or C, which is perfect. You've got them to admit that working with you will get them a good outcome, and now you can move them closer to becoming a client.

## The happiness scale

I love this one. It can be used at any time during the sales process to gauge someone's feelings.

And it's simply asking your prospect this:

'On a scale of 1 to 10 – with 1 being "No, I'm never doing this, I'm out and I never want to see your face again." and 10 being "Yes, sign me up immediately." – where do you sit?'

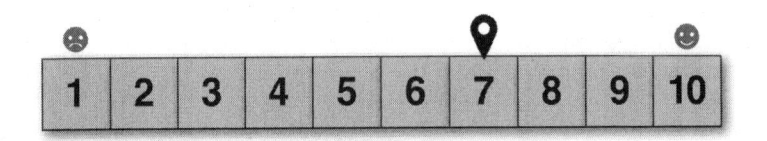

They'll tell you. (Most people usually say six or seven.)

And then you ask, 'Okay, cool. What would make it a 10?'

What they say next will be their true objection and something you have the opportunity to change.

### The comparison principle

All we do here is compare the price of your offer to something that the prospect is already familiar with.

That may be their own offer, splitting the cost across a few months to make the number appear lower or something they already spend money on.

My favourite for C2C is comparing it to the number of clients they need to win in order to make back their initial investment. For example, if your offer is the same as landing two new clients, then the offer pays for itself.

The reason this technique is so powerful is that they're comparing your cost to something they're already familiar with – and it downplays the size of the investment itself.

| A coffee a day | £500 per month | Two new clients |

If you decide to use these techniques, make sure to adapt them to your business and the outcomes your clients are looking for. They work well to reframe and change the way people think because it turns airy-fairy feelings and ideas into something more solid and realistic.

As with everything I've told you, this will take repetition and consistent improvement, so if you use these once and they don't work, just try again.

The more objection scenarios you go through, the less intimidating they are and the easier and more natural they'll become.

## MISTAKES TO AVOID

- ✗ Not using a framework.
- ✗ Believing it's you vs them.
- ✗ Not doing a full discovery phase.
- ✗ Holding yourself back from discussing objections.
- ✗ Not digging deeper to find the true cause of their objection.

## ACTIONS TO TAKE NEXT

- ✓ Practise using the VIPER framework.
- ✓ Try one of the closing techniques on your next call.
- ✓ Watch your sales recordings back to improve your objection handling.
- ✓ Make a list of potential objections your ideal client might have, and plan your responses.

# Sales-Call Roadmap

Download my complete guide to dominating sales calls by scanning the following QR code:

Or by visiting chris-james.co/book-scr

*This is your permission to get out there and take some fucking action.*

# Conclusion

Once you've sold your product or offer, a new journey will begin:

**The paying client's journey.**

Your ability to deliver your offer and provide an experience that exceeds your client's expectations means you'll need different tools and processes to help you along the way.

Unfortunately, there's no time or space for more chapters on onboarding or delivery in this book.

Maybe that'll be the next one?

But until then, when you hit this stage and you've won a few clients or sold a few products, remember this:

**Never take your eyes off the market.**

Without generating leads and converting them, you have no business. Always be mindful of that.

And don't forget these:

- → No leads? Improve your message or marketing.
- → Leads but no clients? Improve your sales skills or revisit your offer.

# Final Thoughts

A lot of people I speak to believe they have to get some form of permission to do something new: to change careers, build a business, sell a new product or be that person they've always wanted to be.

That belief holds them back.

It's fucking nonsense. Don't lie to yourself any longer; this book is your permission:

- → Permission to take an idea, market it and sell it.
- → Permission to ignore all the bullshit you're telling yourself.
- → Permission to go forth and put your *true* self out into the world.

This is your permission to get out there and take some fucking action.

Become that person.

Do it now.

# The Book

*Content to Clients* is designed to help as many people as possible, but the only way to do that is to get more eyeballs on the book itself.

If you found any part of it useful, a review on Amazon would be welcome.

When you do, you'll help the book reach more people who need it too.

—

I'd love to see your progress. Tag me on LinkedIn or Instagram so I can see what you're up to.

Seeing other people succeed truly lights me up. You may have seen some of the client interviews I've done – there have been a few times when the tears came out.

So if *Content to Clients* helps you in any shape or form, please tag me: @ChrisJamesOnline.

# Acknowledgements

I purposely left it right up until the deadline to write this part.

There are far too many people to thank, so here's a really concise list:

- Amy, Ivy, Edward and Ena
- Mum and Dad
- Sara, Sophie, Ol and Russ
- Vicki, Katie and Kathryn
- Rob, Gaz and Adam
- Harrison and Ed Jones
- Zoe Whitman
- All my friends and the people I've met along the way – you know who you are
- All our amazing clients – thank you for the trust
- And younger Chris, thanks for taking action – you should have done it earlier, pal!

# About Me

My first 'sales' job was selling bootleg CDs and tapes at high school. I even sold one to my own science teacher after he caught me listening to Eminem on my Walkman in class.

Today, I use my 15+ years of sales experience to help people earn five-figures a month and land their dream clients online.

I love spending time with my wife Amy, my daughter Ivy and my stepson Edward. I'm obsessed with trainers (the shoes, that is!) and business.

I value hard work and the power of taking action. I hate negativity and love the concept of personal growth.

I believe everyone's got some form of knowledge they can give to the world that'll make it a better place and that they can make money whilst doing it.

This book and my business is my attempt to do exactly that.

It honestly means the world to me to play even the smallest part in changing someone's future – by helping and inspiring people to take action.

Is it my life's calling?

I don't know.

But I fucking love it!

# About Content to Clients (C2C)

Content to Clients (C2C) is a six-month consulting programme that helps small service-based business owners win more clients online using organic content.

It will show you exactly how to do this:

- → Build your offer
- → Market it organically
- → Generate leads quickly
- → Convert them into clients
- → Deliver a world-class service

You'll get access to the following:

- Twice-weekly calls
- Face-to-face events
- C2C's private community
- Guest-expert masterclasses
- C2C's latest course materials
- C2C's exact systems and workflows

Scan the following QR code:

**Content To Clients**

Or visit chris-james.co/c2clp-bk

# References

1. Elon Musk [@elonmusk]. (n.d.). Posts [Twitter/X profile]. Retrieved from: https://twitter.com/elonmusk

2. Tesla [@tesla]. (n.d.). Posts [Twitter/X profile]. Retrieved from: https://twitter.com/Tesla

3. Gary Vaynerchuk [@garyvee]. (n.d.). Posts [Twitter/X profile]. Retrieved from: https://twitter.com/garyvee

4. VaynerMedia [@VaynerMedia]. (n.d.). Posts [Twitter/X profile]. Retrieved from: https://twitter.com/Vaynermedia

5. Richard Branson [@richardbranson]. (n.d.). Posts [Twitter/X profile]. Retrieved from: https://twitter.com/richardbranson

6. Virgin [@Virgin]. (n.d.). Posts [Twitter/X profile]. Retrieved from: https://twitter.com/Virgin

7. Chan Kim, W. and Mauborgne, R.A. (2015). *Blue Ocean Strategy, Expanded Edition: How to create uncontested market space and make the competition irrelevant.* Brighton, MA: Harvard Business Review Press

8. Dewez, A. (2022). *"Crazy until successful" – The MrBeast deep dive* [Blog]. Retrieved from: https://alexandre.substack.com/p/-crazy-until-successful-the-mrbeast

9. Vaynerchuk, G. (2013). *Jab, Jab, Jab, Right Hook: How to tell your story in a noisy social world.* New York, NY: Harper Business.